W9-BLU-298

HOW TO UNDERSTAND YOUR BIBLE

T. NORTON STERRETT

InterVarsity Press
Downers Grove
Illinois 60515

Second printing, October 1976

Revised edition © 1974
by Inter-Varsity Christian Fellowship
of the United States of America.

First edition © 1973
by T. Norton Sterrett.

InterVarsity Press is the
book publishing division of
Inter-Varsity Christian Fellowship,
a student movement active on
campus at hundreds of universities,
colleges and schools of nursing.
For information about local
and regional activities, write
IVCF, 233 Langdon,
Madison, WI 53703.

ISBN 0-87784-638-3
Library of Congress Catalog
Card Number: 74-78674

Printed in the United
States of America

To my coworkers and friends in India
with whom and from whom
I have learned precious truth
in God's Word

Contents

Preface

Suppose a friend sends you a letter which reads, "In general, it is hopeless to expect to be able to define psychic properties in terms of physical properties, and still hold, as Identity theorists do, that it is a factual discovery that C-states and B-processes are identical." If you are like me, to get a message like that would be to get no message at all.

Suppose the letter reads, "Labbayka Allahumma Labbayka." Again, no message.

Perhaps your friend has written this: "In the black, black, a small upper will one, two, three, and bazaar out." Once more, no message.

Each of these three sentences is supposed to communicate, but they have no word for you, because you get no meaning. Two of the sentences use words you know, though the first also has a few unknown ones. The first, however, is apparently in some branch of knowledge you have not studied. Perhaps an expert in that field could give you the meaning. The second is in another language, so you would have to study that language or ask a translator to give you the message. The third uses simple, familiar words, but if it has any meaning it apparently is a hidden, mystical one, perhaps connected with magic or the occult and understood only through a special experience.

Many people, even some Christians, regard the Bible as you regard these three sentences: It is a message from God, written mainly in words you know, but with a meaning that is generally not clear. So, they say, you need an expert to explain it to you—a pastor, perhaps, or some Bible scholar. Or you need a long course of study that will enable you to understand its meaning. Maybe the Bible is a hidden, divine writing you can understand only through a special experience.

If you view the Bible in any of these ways, then you will not study it. You may read a short portion in the morning for a Quiet Time and not worry about the non-sense verses you have to skip over. But you will not attempt more study, for you do not have time to take a long course and you think that anything less will not do much good. So for you the Word of God is mainly unknown: It is a word that does not communicate.

Does this make sense? Why should God speak to the church in such a way that most of the people cannot understand it? The answer is that he did not do that. Christians *can* understand the Bible. It is not necessary to wait for an expert or to take a lengthy theological course or to have some strange, mystical experience that other Christians do not have.

No, you can understand the Bible, if you *will*. It is up to you. Do you want to learn? How eager are you? Answer that question before you go any farther. If you are determined to learn the Bible, to set aside a regular time, say a half-hour each day, and give that time to the prayerful study of the Bible, God will teach you. And then this book can help you in practical ways to know how to study.

This book is divided into four sections. The *first* takes up some basic matters: what interpretation is, why it is necessary, what you need to be an interpreter, what tools you will want and how to undertake this task. The *second* discusses the general principles for interpreting Bible language, principles that we use with all kinds of language (like paying attention to the context). The *third* examines principles that apply to special types of language, such as parables, figures of speech and prophecy. The *fourth* considers how to apply the Bible to our own lives—how to know what God is saying to us personally and what we should do about it.

Bible quotations are from the Revised Standard Version unless otherwise noted. Where the Authorized Version is quoted it is referred to as the AV.

I
Basic Considerations

1

Personal Bible Study Is a Must

The Bible is God's Word to us. As Christians we believe God has given us this wonderful gift to treasure, to keep, to learn, to understand and to obey. But we cannot fulfill these purposes if our Bible remains closed and hidden away, or if we do not understand what it says. God's Word is for all of us. It should light our way. It should be our daily bread.

Feeding is more than drinking a coke, ready-mixed by someone else. It often requires hard biting and chewing. Likewise, feeding on God's Word often requires hard studying, observing, thinking, working. Nor should we limit this feeding to once a week, in a Sunday morning service. It is not enough simply to take food from someone else after he has worked over it, eliminated some of the harder parts and extracted some soft, nutritious bites. Neither occasional nor second-hand dining is adequate.

Perhaps you have already tried to study the Bible, but without much success. So you gave up, and settled only for a brief Quiet Time, a few minutes each day to read a short portion, get help from some notes, find a "thought for the day" and spend a short time in prayer. You now look for obvious promises or commands, but anything difficult you pass over. Yet you sense this is unsatisfactory and have a feeling that God wants you to get much more from the Bible.

You are right. God commands us to learn his Word (Ps. 119:9, 11). Furthermore, God tells us that we *can* understand the Word. The apostle John writes to believers, "You have no need that anyone should teach you" (1 Jn. 2:27). He asserts that the believer has the Holy Spirit ("anointing") as his teacher (see also v. 20). So, because you have a divine teacher, you can understand God's truth.

This does not mean that God will teach us without our doing something. God feeds the birds, as Jesus said, but the birds work hard to get that food. God has promised to feed us on his Word. Our job is to study. The food is there and we can get it. This is one of the tremendous blessings of the Christian life!

Human Teachers

But, you may ask, doesn't God provide teachers for the church, men who explain the Word of God to other Christians? Yes, the Bible states clearly that God gives some people the gift and ministry of teaching (1 Cor. 12:28; Eph. 4:11). But that is only one phase of God's arrangement for understanding his Word. The other is the one stated in John—that each believer should also learn from the Holy Spirit.

This does not mean that we ignore or despise the teachers God has placed in the church. We cannot understand everything by ourselves; we must learn with and from others. God places in the church people who are gifted to expound the Scriptures and explain the great doctrines of the faith, and we are to listen to them receptively and prayerfully. Even then, we are to confirm their teaching, not just accept it blindly. The Jews at Beroea were commended because they not only listened receptively to Paul but also verified from the Scriptures the truth of his message (Acts 17:11).

Young Christians, especially, need to consult older Christians who know the Word of God and can help them understand it. If you have studied a portion of the Bible and feel you have discovered some new truth, talk over your idea with a more mature believer; new ideas are not always right, even those which come from prayerful study. After sharing with a mature friend, study the passage again, considering carefully any counsel he has given you.

The Teaching of the Holy Spirit

God uses the human teachers, and he uses our own prayerful study. But we cannot expect to understand God's Word by these alone. God the Holy Spirit must be our Teacher. Christ himself said, "He [the Holy Spirit] will guide you into all the truth" and "He will teach you all things" (Jn. 16:13; 14:26). God who inspired the writing of this Word has promised to guide us so that we know what it means. What an encouragement to spur us on to read and study the Bible!

This is a blessed truth for *all* Christians: God has sent his Holy Spirit to dwell in *every* believer; our bodies are his temple (1 Cor. 6:19). One of the main things the Spirit has come to do is to illuminate the Scriptures. If we recognize his teaching ministry, we shall be stimulated and stirred to dig into the Bible.

We will also be guarded against two wrong attitudes toward Bible knowledge. First, we will not place any confidence in ourselves. We will not think that our minds can grasp biblical truth unaided, that our hard study gives us a special and expert knowledge or that what we know of the Bible is final. We will have a humble spirit, thanking God for all that we do know but recognizing that there is still much more to learn. The man who must have known more of God's Word than any other of his time was inspired by God to write these words of counsel, "If any one imagines that he knows something, he does not yet know as he ought to know" (1 Cor. 8:2). The apostle Paul was not referring to math or science but to things pertaining to God. We have no ground for deadly pride in our knowledge of the Bible.

Second, we will not fail to have confidence in the Lord to give us knowledge of his Word. We will accept the Spirit's teaching without doubt or disbelief. If pride is deadly, so is unbelief. Think of learning from God! We should never take this privilege lightly.

Yet some Christians draw the wrong conclusion from this privilege. They feel that if the Holy Spirit is our teacher then we need not study. All we have to do, they say, is get down on our knees and read the Bible prayerfully, asking God to teach us. Then the thoughts and convictions which come to us are from God. This, they say, is what it means to feed on the Word of God. Diligent study is unnecessary.

We recognize that we must read the Word of God prayerfully, seeking the teaching of the Holy Spirit, and we know that God gives understanding in answer to prayer, but it is a mistake to conclude that Bible study is unnecessary. God gave the Israelites water from a rock when Moses struck it with his rod, but this was exceptional. God required Abraham and Jacob to do the hard work of digging wells. The water came *from* God in answer to prayer, and *through* hard work. We must not let our natural tendency to avoid work and hard thinking deceive us.

God can give both supernaturally or naturally. He has given us minds with which to understand him, and he asks us to *cleanse* them and *use* them. We are to "gird up" our minds (1 Pet. 1:13) and to love the Lord with all our mental ability (Mt. 22:37).

Adequate But Not Perfect Understanding

Saying that we can understand God's Word does not mean we can understand everything in it, solve all problems of interpretation and get answers to all our questions. The precise meaning of some things seems to be still secret. Even scholars who know Greek and Hebrew, cultural and historical background, and so forth, are unable to explain satisfactorily some verses. For instance, there are many inter-pretations of being "baptized on behalf of the dead" (1 Cor. 15:29), but no Bible student can be sure just what it means. Christ's preaching to the spirits in prison (1 Pet. 3:19) is another puzzle on which scholars do not agree.

But we need not be upset by this. We can understand enough to know God's will and to obey his commands. We must persist and get what God has for us. While we are not sure what it meant to be baptized for the dead, we can sup-pose that Paul's readers at Corinth knew. And whatever it meant, it was something that would not make sense without a resurrection of the dead. That is the meaning of the verse: It is one more evidence for the resurrection. And that is what we need to know.

God encourages us to study his Word, promising that he will enable us to understand it and to fellowship with him in its light. But he does not tell us that knowledge will come easily. If we are not serious, we may as well not think of studying the Bible. But if we are serious, we have great blessing ahead. We can have no greater riches than to learn precious truth in the Word of God and so get to know God more and more.

The truth we get from the Word ourselves, rather than from speakers or writers, is doubly precious. I remember the joy I experienced when I received new light on a puz-zling verse, "But many that are first will be last, and the last first" (Mt. 19:30). I spent some time studying both the state-ment and its context, and finally understanding came. Not only did I feel joyful, but God rebuked and challenged me with the truth that the last laborers in the parable became first and the first last because of their attitudes, depending on whether self-interest was dominant or not. The work I expended on this study was more than worthwhile.

So if you desire to study the Bible, read on. The first six chapters (Section I) are intended to help you understand some important things that affect Bible study. The chapters

that follow them deal first with general principles of interpretation (Section II), then specific ones (Section III) and
finally application (Section IV).

2

Who Can Understand the Bible?

Not everyone can properly interpret the Bible. Its main truth is spiritual, so only the spiritually qualified can understand it. God's Word is for people who can and will listen.

Every true Christian already has some of the necessary qualifications. Others he may acquire. Without them he has no chance of knowing the Bible properly. Let us consider what these qualities are.

1. *A new heart* (1 Cor. 2:14). The interpreter must be born again. The Bible message concerns God and man and their relationship. Therefore, one who stands outside that relationship will miss much of what God has said. He may be able to accumulate many facts and comprehend technical points of language. If he is a scholar, he may be able to acquire much knowledge about the Bible, its history, its people and even some of its teachings. But the man who has not received spiritual life from God lacks an essential qualification for understanding God's message.

2. *A hungry heart* (1 Pet. 2:2). Bible knowledge does not come through casual interest and occasional reading. It is not like pretty colored stones lying on the seashore that you can pick up in a few minutes any time you wish. Rather, it is like precious ore in a mine; you can find it only if you are determined to get it. Such determination comes when you

are eager to know God and his Word.

Imagine a believer who, having some desire to know God's Word, decides to study it. One morning he gets up a little earlier than usual, makes a cup of coffee and sits down to study. After asking God for help, he begins to read; but a few minutes later, he feels sleepy. He has not yet found some wonderful truth or "received a blessing," so, tired and disappointed, he either goes back to bed or turns to something else, like the newspaper, the radio or a book. Or perhaps he tries to find some commentary or notes to give him a spiritual thought.

Where was this Christian's hunger for God? If he had any, it was easily satisfied. Other seemingly more interesting things caused him to close his Bible. He may have fooled himself and said, "I tried to study but I can't understand." Actually he read only as long as he did not have to try. When he found that effort was needed, he gave up. There was no insatiable hunger that kept him going. A man without a hungry heart can never learn the Bible.

3. *An obedient heart* (Ps. 119:98-100). To understand the Bible truly we must be willing to obey what God shows us of his will. The Bible calls for response, not just analysis. If we are unwilling to act, we cannot reach the full truth. A disobedient heart means a closed understanding. An obedient heart finds the meaning of the Scripture opened.

God requires this heart attitude, not a perfect record of action. He does not wait until we have followed him perfectly for some length of time before he instructs us from his Word. No, he sees our heart and knows whether it is responsive. If it is, then he is ready to teach us.

Learning and obedience go together, step by step. If God teaches me something and I obey, I can expect God to teach me more. If I refuse to obey, then I should not expect to progress even in knowledge. I may acquire more facts, but the essential spiritual truth will be hidden. I may get the bulk content of the rice and curry, but will not assimilate the hidden, health-giving vitamins. Without obedience at each step, further steps in knowing God's Word are impossible.

4. *A disciplined heart* (Mt. 7:7). A person with a disciplined heart will start something and keep on doing it, even though it is hard. He will cut out other things he would like to do for the sake of a higher priority. Though he may need a long time to accomplish the task, he will not be drawn away, because he knows it is right. Learning the Bible requires such a heart.

And the discipline must be self-discipline. No one else can compel a man to study the Bible. At times we will find Bible study very interesting, even thrilling, but not always. On some days new truths will excite us, but on other days they will not. Yet if we are disciplined, we will press on because the goal is not reached quickly or easily.

Many Christians have started Bible courses. They have done one, two or three lessons, found that these take time from other things and are not always thrilling, and so have given up. If that is our way, there is no use seeking to learn God's Word or beginning a definite study program. Jesus said, "Seek and you will find," not "You will find by chance or a casual look."

5. *A teachable heart* (Is. 50:4). The teachable heart wants to learn and to go on learning. It never says, "Now I know enough." Rather, it knows it has much more to understand, and eagerly and humbly is ready to discover new truth at any time.

Also, it is ready to acquire knowledge from others. Perhaps we are willing to learn from God, or think we are, but are we willing to be taught by another brother or sister, especially if the brother is right and I am mistaken? This test will reveal the teachable heart.

We all have ideas about Scripture, convictions regarding doctrine and the meaning of many passages. Where did we get these ideas? Most of them have come from messages we have heard, books we have read, thoughts we have gained from others. Some of our convictions may be right; some may be wrong, or only partly right. Are we willing to say, "I may be wrong"? If not, then our heart is not fully teachable. It is not open to the instruction of the Lord, even though we study the Bible with great zeal.

The humble, teachable heart is the one to whom God shows his truth.

These five spiritual qualities are important if we want to understand the Bible. The more we have them, the more we can learn. If we want them, we should ask God for them, and we should begin studying the Bible even as we pray. If we study with a seeking, prayerful attitude, we will be where God can teach us. And he will.

3

The Importance of Proper Understanding

Bible students have thought, studied and written a great deal about how to interpret the Bible. Such work is necessary, for proper interpretation is an urgent matter.

Many verses are not clear to us. We read them once, then again, then again, and still we are puzzled. We can see two (or more) possible meanings. "It might mean this or it might mean that," we say. Sometimes a verse is so puzzling that we cannot see even one possible meaning. In either case we realize we need interpretation to make the meaning clear.

Two Hard Verses

Consider, for example, this statement: "Be not unequally yoked together with unbelievers" (2 Cor. 6:14, AV). What does this verse mean? A yoke is a wooden bar laid across the necks of two draft animals (like oxen) to link them for doing some work, such as pulling a plow. Does this verse say that a believer should not get under such a wooden bar alongside of someone who is not a Christian? That would be nonsense.

Does it refer to the marriage of a believer with an unbeliever? Or does it forbid a believer to take a business partner who is an unbeliever? Or does it forbid a Christian to join societies such as the Masons or Rotary, where membership is mixed? What *is* "the unequal yoke"? And how can we find out?

What about this statement in the Psalms: "The dead do not praise the Lord" (Ps. 115:17)? Don't believers worship God even after they die? Do we have a clear idea of what this sentence means?

These two verses, and many others, need interpretation, but how shall we arrive at the true meaning? As we think about a verse, some idea may come to mind, but you may have one thought and I another. How can we decide which one is correct? This is the problem of interpretation.

Communicating with Each Other

We use language for communication. When one man wants to communicate with another, he speaks, writes, sings or acts to make his meaning clear. In all but the latter he uses words. If the other person correctly understands the meaning of the language, then there is communication.

But often we misunderstand each other. The first time I heard someone say, "You're pulling my leg," I did not know what he meant, and what he seemed to mean was not very nice. Now I know that this is a figure of speech, which simply means, "You're joking." So for understanding one another as well as for understanding the Bible, we need to understand language.

There are principles to guide us in understanding language, and many of these apply to Bible study. There are also a few special principles concerning Bible language. In any branch of knowledge we have to learn both theory and practice, and it is much the same in interpreting the Bible. The study of the principles of interpretation is called *hermeneutics*. The practice of these principles is called *exegesis* or *interpretation*. When one person passes on his interpretation to others, this is called *exposition*. In this book we are considering the principles first but are also trying to see how they are applied.

The Importance of Correct Principles

Suppose someone is reading Acts 15:28-29 and notes that the question being discussed concerns salvation. Now he reads that the church leaders sent a message to the new Gentile Christians at Antioch about certain "necessary things": "abstain from what has been sacrificed to idols and from blood [in meat] and from what is strangled and from unchastity." Suppose the reader concludes that one is saved just by abstaining from these things.

He may also read in James, "You see that a man is justified by works and not by faith alone" (Jas. 2:24). This reinforces his conclusion that he can be saved by works, and he builds his life on that belief, thus misunderstanding God's Word and the way of salvation. His destiny depends on his interpreting these Scriptures correctly. While we have only supposed that someone might make this mistake, the sad fact is that many actually do.

To interpret the Bible correctly we must use correct principles of interpretation. We do not have the right to make up our own or to use any ones we like. So how do we get them? One way is to study how the New Testament interprets the Old. Another way (since the Bible is written in human language) is to study *the laws of language,* the principles for understanding language generally.

For example, imagine a man saying, "My friend strikes out in everything he tries." Some people will have no idea what he is talking about. Others will think he is discussing a baseball game because that is what the words *describe.* But if the man has just been telling how his friend always gets into difficulties in his business and then makes this statement about striking out, people know he is not talking about athletics but is using a figure of speech to describe vividly a man in trouble. We know the meaning of the sentence by the rest of the man's speech. This is a law of language called *context,* and it is a basic principle of biblical interpretation.

Several principles of biblical interpretation are simply general laws of language. The Bible itself highlights a good number of them. For example, Jesus told his disciples to beware of the leaven of the Pharisees (Mt. 16:6-12). They took this literally and misunderstood him, so he had to explain that he was using *leaven* to mean "teaching." This is a figure of speech called a metaphor. Jesus used the same kind of language when he said, "Destroy this temple." (Jn. 2:19-22), using *temple* to refer to his own body.

Thus it is clear that while every believer has the right to interpret the Bible for himself, he has no right to make up his own private rules. He cannot decide that *house* means *bazaar* and maintain that every time someone speaks of a house he is talking about a bazaar. To do that would destroy language as a way of communicating between persons. No, the Holy Spirit has inspired the writing of the Bible in human language; therefore, that language is to be understood by the laws of language, especially as they are revealed in the Bible itself.

4

The
Point
of
Departure

Every activity must have a starting point. In Bible study we start with our convictions about the Bible and about the proper approach to its study. I will not try to prove these, but will state them here.

Some people tell us we should not do this. They say we should come to the Bible with an open mind, with no convictions about whether it is God's Word or whether it is true. We should, according to them, study the Bible and see what it proves itself to be. If it is God's Word, it will show itself to be such.

That is a possible way to study the Bible, but not the approach I shall use in this book. For one thing, it is impossible to have a completely open mind. Anyone who knows something about the Bible has some convictions. In the second place, such an approach would require a book much too large for our purpose. And third, Bible scholars have already used this approach and have thoroughly and competently set forth the evidence that the Bible is from God.

Our Basic Convictions
So we will begin from certain fundamental convictions, which are the foundations of this study. All evangelical

Christians will agree with those that relate to what the Bible is. Those that concern the approach to Bible study may not be shared by all, but I hope to show that they are reasonable.

1. *The Bible (both Old and New Testaments) is God's Word.* It is inspired by God and therefore different from all other books. To put it simply, what the Bible says God says. To understand the Bible truly, you must be confident that it is God's Word, through which he has spoken to human beings, including you. You must affirm that the Bible's statements are authoritative and trustworthy, that you can depend on them without question.

This conviction is basic to our study of the Bible and affects our whole approach. For Bible study is not just a technique. The attitude of faith is vital for understanding. If you have doubts on this matter you should get them cleared up before you begin studying. Ask God to show you the truth and then read some helpful books on this subject. I recommend the following: *Christ and the Bible* by John Wenham (InterVarsity Press); *Authority* by Martyn Lloyd-Jones (InterVarsity Press); and *Biblical Revelation* by Clark Pinnock (Moody Press).

We need to be careful here, however. God may not say what someone *thinks* the Bible says. Many people have silly or wild ideas. Just because we believe the Bible does not mean that all our ideas are necessarily correct or that our understanding of a particular verse is right. That is one of the main reasons we need to interpret carefully.

2. *The Bible can be adequately understood in the translations.* Some Christians believe that only by studying the Bible in Hebrew and Greek can we get the meaning adequately, but most believers through most of the time since Christ have known the Bible only in translation. Even today, only a tiny minority of Christians in the world have the opportunity to read the writings of scholars who know the original languages. Commentaries, concordances and other study helps are either not available in most languages or are too

costly. Does God arrange things so that most Christians cannot adequately know his Word? No, translations do convey the essential meaning of the Bible.

This does not mean that scholarship is useless. It is important and valuable. Through scholarship, we gain additional knowledge and valuable insights, especially into difficult problems of interpretation. But you can study the translation you have and expect to gain real understanding.

The Bible, of course, was not written originally in the language that most people have as their mother tongue. The Old Testament came in Hebrew (except for small portions in Aramaic), the New Testament in Greek. So the Bibles we use are translations, whether English, Hindi, Tamil, Spanish or Chinese. Most translations have been made carefully and prayerfully by godly Christian scholars, and we can have confidence in these translations. One example is a translation of the Old Testament into Greek, made about 280 B.C., called the *Septuagint.* The New Testament frequently quotes from this rather than from the original Hebrew (or at least from the same Hebrew text that exists today). Matthew 13:14-15; Luke 3:4-6; and Romans 15:12 are examples of such passages.

Not all translations have been made carefully, however, and some have been made by those who do not have full confidence in the inspiration of the Scriptures. So you need to know the translations you use. This is more necessary in English than in most other languages because of the number of translations available.

3. *The Bible is a unity.* The Old and New Testaments do not contradict each other in their revelation of God. Rather, the two are complementary: The Old prepares for the New and the New fulfills the Old.

There is progress in the revelation: The Old Testament is partial and given "in many various ways," while the final revelation, recorded in the New Testament, is through Christ. Christ, however, is the center of the Old Testament, too, though his portrait there is in parts and pieces. We shall understand the Bible only as we see in the whole of it Christ and God's plan of redemption through him. (See Chapter 21.)

4. *The Bible is its own interpreter.* That is, one passage throws light on another. Comparing Scripture with Scripture is basic in biblical interpretation. Plain statements help explain obscure ones. Literal statements illumine figurative ones. New Testament history and teaching unveil Old Testament prophecy.

Such comparing is to be done carefully, not arbitrarily. For instance, a man may read that "whoever of you does not renounce all that he has cannot be my disciple" (Lk. 14:33). Comparing that with the command to "sell all that you have and distribute to the poor ... and come, follow me" (Lk. 18:22), he decides to get rid of all his possessions, despite the fact that he has a wife and five children. Having done this, he can no longer take care of his family and has to depend on the charity of others. This man made a superficial comparison of Scripture with Scripture. He did not take into account 1 Corinthians 16:2; 1 Timothy 5:8; 6:17-19; and other passages.

We must look carefully to Scripture itself to give us light for understanding it. (See Chapter 12.)

5. *The Bible language is mainly normal human language.* At one time it was thought that the New Testament was written in a heavenly or spiritual Greek, but later it was learned that the New Testament language is the ordinary language of the first century A.D. The language was affected by the culture of the Jewish people of that time, and so the New Testament contains many expressions peculiar to the Jews (Hebrew idioms—which we will examine in Chapter 17). There are some words that had a common meaning but in the Bible were given a special meaning, *ecclesia* (church) and *agapao* (to love), for example. Prophetic language has special characteristics, such as speaking of a future event in

the past tense.

In the main, though, the Bible writers used ordinary language—nouns, verbs and so forth. Even many of its figures of speech are like ours. When the Bible speaks of trees clapping their hands or hills laughing, we have no difficulty understanding this. We can expect to find the elements of language we already know and to apply the ordinary laws of language.

6. *Our understanding of the Bible must be accompanied by an honest, intelligent and obedient response to its message.* The Word of God is given so that "the man of God may be complete, equipped for every good work" (2 Tim. 3:17). No understanding of the Bible is simply technical and theoretical. When a truth is clear to the mind, the will must respond. Knowledge and obedience cannot be separated. We learn in order that we may do, and we have not truly learned until we do.

7. *The Holy Spirit's teaching is necessary for understanding the Bible.* "He will guide you into all the truth," said Jesus, referring to the Holy Spirit (Jn. 16:13). Spiritual things "are spiritually discerned," said Paul (1 Cor. 2:14). The truths of the Bible go beyond the facts and information found in it. The basic meaning of the Bible is spiritual, and to get that meaning we must be taught by the Holy Spirit.

The seven convictions listed above provide, I believe, an indispensable basis for understanding the Bible. Now we will consider tools we should have on hand as we begin our work.

5

Using
the
Right
Tools

Most people probably think that reference books like commentaries and Bible dictionaries are necessary tools for Bible study. No doubt they are helpful, for they give us the insights of Bible scholars. But many Christians, especially those in poorer circumstances, cannot have these helps. Must they wait to study the Bible until they can get them? If so, many would have to wait forever.

Besides, there is a definite harm in using reference books the wrong way—particularly by substituting them for personal study. This is like eating pre-chewed or pre-digested food. No doubt we can get some benefit from such food, but think of what we miss: the benefit to the body of doing our own chewing, the enjoyment of good-tasting food, etc. In Bible study the loss that comes from simply reading what others have learned is even greater. No blessing and joy can surpass what we get from studying the Bible and learning directly from the Lord.

The Scofield Reference Bible is an example of an aid that many Christians use. The disadvantage of using it as a study Bible is that the notes may easily replace personal reflection. These notes are not part of the inspired Word of God, and many Bible students believe some of them are misleading.

In order not to miss the benefit of your own study, use other books *after* you have done your work, not before. They are helpful especially in giving information you cannot get from the Bible alone, for example, additional facts about people and places. And they provide useful comments on passages that are difficult to understand.

The Basic Tools

If, then, we cannot consider reference books as indispensable tools for Bible study, what are the basic tools we need?

1. *A basic study Bible.* In one sense, of course, the Bible is not a tool for Bible study: It is what we are studying. However, we will consider the choice of a Bible along with the tools. Get a Bible with marginal cross references, and one with margins wide enough and paper thick enough for writing notes. If you prefer not to mark in your Bible, make sure you have a notebook handy.

Which version is best? The King James, or Authorized, Version has been the standard English Bible for the last 360 years (since 1611), but it is difficult today to understand it since the English language has changed. There are many words and expressions in the AV that themselves now need translation! Certain editions provide notes to clear up these difficulties, but, even then, much of the language tends to be foreign. So if you use the AV, you will have an added (and unnecessary) difficulty in understanding God's Word, and you should surely have a recent translation for comparison.

The Revised Standard Version is another one to consider. Its up-to-date language is easier to understand than the AV. Some Christians feel, however, that it reflects a freer treatment of the original languages and therefore is questionable. One way to guard against this is to have both the AV and RSV. Use one of them as your study Bible and compare it with the other.

2. *Other Bible translations or paraphrases for comparison.*

Have one or two for this purpose, but not a great many. Too many will be confusing. Do all the versions agree? Why do they differ? Which do I prefer? It will seem too much like trying to solve a puzzle.

There are many new translations and paraphrases, such as J. B. Phillips', the Today's English Version, the Living Bible and the New English Bible. These all have weaknesses, but they succeed in bringing the Word to life through modern language. We should use them.

3. *A language dictionary.* Everyone knows his mother tongue, but not perfectly. A dictionary helps in several ways. It enables us to understand clearly and precisely the meaning of words we are acquainted with but cannot define. It suggests meanings to words we do not know. Often it corrects us when we think we know the meaning of a word but are mistaken.

The value of a dictionary is limited, however. Since it is concerned with the way people today generally use the words, it does not normally give the exact meaning of a word as the Bible uses it. And since it gives all the meanings of each word, not just one, you have to decide for yourself which is the biblical meaning.

Make use of a desk dictionary in your Bible study, and do not pass over words you do not know. If you do not have a dictionary at hand while studying, write down unknown words and look them up as soon as you can. We will discuss further the use of a dictionary in a later chapter (Chapter 8).

4. *A notebook.* If you do not write things down, your study can never be what it should be. First, when you take notes you see more, and second, you remember more. Sometimes writing may seem tedious and tiring, but do not give way to laziness.

What should you note? First, facts—repeated words, special or unusual things, people and places. Even if a fact seems unimportant, note it. You may see its significance later. Second, references to other passages. As you read, you may recall a verse somewhere else that seems to connect with what you have just read. Third, questions that come to your mind. Do not stop to try to answer them, but be sure to record them. Fourth, thoughts and interpretations.

In your first readings, it is good to note almost everything that comes to your mind as you read, without stopping to analyze or check each idea. Perhaps a large portion of it may not be meaningful in the end, but you do not know in the beginning what is and what is not significant. Later you can review your initial comments, sort things out, make further notes and draw conclusions.

Other Tools

I have mentioned above the basic tools needed for Bible study. Now I will mention some of the reference books which, while not indispensable, are helpful. It is good to secure them if you can.

1. *Concordance.* A concordance lists the verses in which a particular word is used. Smaller concordances, like Cruden's, list the main occurrences of a word but not all of them, especially for those words that occur hundreds of times. The complete concordances, like *Young's Analytical Concordance* and *Strong's Exhaustive Concordance,* list all or nearly all of the times every word occurs in the Bible. They are based on the AV. *Nelson's Complete Concordance* is available for the RSV.

A concordance is especially helpful for word study, when you want to find out where and how a word is used throughout the whole Bible. We will consider later the advantages and disadvantages of such study.

2. *Bible dictionary.* A Bible dictionary lists and explains words and subjects found in the Bible. It summarizes the biblical meanings but does not necessarily give many references. It tells, for instance, how many people in the Bible were named John and who they were. It provides informa-

tion about historical and cultural background. It treats some subjects, like archaeology and the Trinity, even though the actual word is not found in the Bible. It usually does not explain individual verses, as a commentary does. While a concordance gives only factual information (about where words are found), a Bible dictionary, like a commentary, gives the opinion of the author. The best Bible dictionary in one volume is the *New Bible Dictionary* (Inter-Varsity Press and Eerdmans).

3. *Commentary.* A commentary gives the author's opinion about the meaning of the actual text of Scripture, book by book, chapter by chapter, sometimes even verse by verse. Some are very thorough; others are brief, giving only summaries of paragraphs or chapters. Helpful background or introductory material on each book, such as author, date and place of writing, and occasion for writing, is usually given, along with an outline or summary of the contents. It is probably the most practical and helpful to add to your library first a one volume commentary on the whole Bible. The *New Bible Commentary* (InterVarsity Press and Eerdmans) is one of the best.

The Use of the Tools
A man uses tools to help him work more effectively, but he himself does the work. So the tools for Bible interpretation are designed to help the interpreter do the work; they do not do his work for him. What you learn yourself means more to you and will be remembered better than what someone else tells you. Suppose you have some math problems to solve. It is easier to get an expert to work them for you, but you do not learn much that way. Nor do you get the joy that comes from your own discovery.

Of course there may be an occasional math problem for which you must have help. Similarly, it is good to use reference books to get information you cannot get otherwise or to help with an occasional interpretation problem. God's

Word says that we are to "comprehend with all the saints" (Eph. 3:18), and so in the body of Christ we need to learn from one another. It is good to read the writings of godly men and counsel with them about the meaning of the Word after we have done some study ourselves.

We have listed seven tools to use in learning God's Word. Some are necessary. Others are helpful but not essential. You may already have some or all of them. Good tools or many tools do not of themselves produce good study, for they depend on the spirit and work of the one who is using them. The knowledge and blessing you get from your study will not come because you have three Bibles and a concordance. They will come because you whole-heartedly and prayerfully give yourself to learning the Bible and because you obediently follow God as he leads you step by step.

How to Proceed

6

We have talked so far about general matters, foundational things that are important for those who want to study the Bible. Now we will get down to some specific suggestions for the actual study. How shall we start? What shall we do?

1. *Plan your study.* You can jump from one short passage to another, but that does not help you know the Bible as you ought to. You must plan your study to get the most from it. There are many good plans. One is to study a book at a time, alternating between Old and New Testaments. Since each was written separately, the books are the natural units of the Bible.

If you have done little Bible study so far, you will be wise not to start with one of the longer books or one of the more difficult ones. Do not, for instance, begin with Isaiah. The Gospels, on the other hand, are good starting points. (Because Mark is the shortest, I will use illustrations from it in this chapter.) One of the shorter New Testament Epistles would also be a good jumping off place, say, 1 John or Philippians. The important thing is to plan your study.

When you have chosen a book, then decide on shorter study portions. A good length is 20 to 25 verses. Many Bibles have paragraph divisions, and these can help. You can use longer sections in the Gospels and shorter ones in the Epistles. It may seem better to choose full chapters, but sometimes you find rather long ones and occasionally the chapter division is not the natural break in thought. But there is nothing rigid about the choice of a portion.

For example, chapter 1 of Mark has 45 verses, about twice as many as we would like to cover. The paragraph division comes naturally after verse 20, so we take verses 1-20 as our first portion.

2. *Pray concerning your study.* Ask God to teach you through his Holy Spirit. Knowing that unless God teaches you your study will be fruitless, you will want to pray even before planning the study and before each day's work. You will also want to pray whenever you come up against a difficult problem or feel confused. Thank God when he gives light and blesses your heart with some new insight. When you think of applying the truth, seeking to know what you are to do, you will sense a need for prayer. Thus, prayer undergirds the whole study—from beginning to end.

3. *Read.* It is good to read the entire book at least once or twice before starting the study of any portion of it. The Gospel of Mark may seem long, but you can read it in one evening or during an hour or two in the afternoon. The benefit you will get will repay the difficulty of finding sufficient time: The view of the whole book will be of great help in understanding the individual portions. After studying three or four sections, read the entire book again. You will be surprised how much this helps open the book to your understanding.

Each time you study, read and reread the selected portion. The more times you read, the more benefit you will get. You will see things on the fifth reading that you did not see before—and even more on the tenth. One of the greatest weaknesses in the Bible study of many Christians is that they want understanding before getting acquainted with the passage. They want to know what God means before they know what he has said. So they read a passage through once, probably in a hurry, then try to figure out what it means. God's words should be given proper respect. We must read them over and over again to fix them in our mind.

During your first reading, or first few readings, do not stop to interpret. You can observe and make notes (in fact, it is good to take notes throughout the study), but do not stop initially to delve into the meaning. First become thoroughly familiar with what the passage says.

4. *Observe.* Reading can be careless. It is easy to read without noticing, not taking in what you read. Lack of observation is especially common in Bible reading. It is similar to what happens when people meet some famous person, like the President. At such a time many are so flustered by knowing they are in the presence of someone important that they do not observe his appearance. It is vital, however, to observe carefully what is in the Bible. Your understanding depends on it; for if you do not know what is said you can never know what is meant.

What kind of things should you observe? Let us take examples from Mark 1:1-20.

a. *The literary form of the passage.* Is it narrative, poetry, didactic (teaching), prophecy, etc.? For example, verses 1-3 are introduction, verses 4-20, narrative. Noting the form is important because each form of language (parallelism in Hebrew poetry, for instance) has features that require special interpretation. I will discuss this and other features later.

b. *Repeated words and phrases.* For instance, *gospel* is found in verses 1, 14, 15; *preaching* in verses 4, 7, 14; *repent/repentance* in verses 4, 15; *immediately (straightway)* in verses 10, 12, 18, 20. Some of these repetitions may be significant, some may not. You can find out later as you continue your study, but note them first.

c. *Connectives or linking words.* Examples are *and, but, for, since, therefore, when* and *after.* Each of them has a special force in connecting words or sentences, and that affects the meaning.

In verses 4-20, eleven of the verses begin with *and.* This conjunction is common in narrative and gives no problem in understanding. It simply indicates that events followed one after the other. Sometimes, however, much meaning depends on the linking word. Suppose I say, "Paul eats a lot of candy *because* he is fat." Or, "Paul eats a lot of candy, *therefore* he is fat." The meaning of the two sentences is quite different, though the amount of candy and Paul's weight may be the same in both cases. In Mark 1 *but* in the middle of verse 8 is significant. *But* almost always shows contrast. Does it show that here?

d. *Time words.* These are found especially in narrative. They include such words as *after, then, immediately, before, at evening* and *one hour later.* Specifically in Mark we see *immediately* (vv. 10, 12, 18, 20); *when* (v. 10); *in those days* (v. 9); and *after* (v. 14).

e. *Location, or place, words.* Examples are *Judea* (v. 5); *Nazareth* (v. 9); *Sea of Galilee* (v. 16).

f. *Contrasts and comparisons. My messenger* is contrasted with *the Lord* (vv. 2-3); *tempted by Satan* with *the angels ministered to him* (v. 13); *Son of God* can be compared with *my beloved Son* (vv. 1, 11); and John's preaching to Jesus' preaching (vv. 7, 14).

g. *Unknown words.* You can look these up in a standard dictionary, except for some Bible names. There may be no unknown words in the Mark passage since narrative usually has fewer such words. But, in the AV, notice *remission* (v. 4) and *latchet* (v. 7).

h. *The core of each sentence.* In long and involved sentences it is well to note the subject, the main verb and the object of the verb (if any). In Mark 1:14-15, "Jesus came . . . preaching . . . and saying" is the core of the sentence. The rest of the sentence answers questions about it. When did

Jesus preach? after John was arrested. What did he preach? the gospel. What did he say? the time is fulfilled, etc.

Again, narrative language is usually simpler so there may be no problem here. In the prophetic books and the epistles, though, there are long, complicated sentences that are not easy to sort out. (See Eph. 1:3-12, AV.)

i. *Figurative expressions.* We will discuss these more fully later. (See Chapter 13.) Some are difficult to understand, others easy. Examples of figurative expressions in Mark are *the thong of whose sandals I am not worthy to stoop down and untie* (v. 7), *at hand* (v. 15) and *I will make you to become fishers of men* (v. 17).

j. *Logical sequences.* Often two items in a passage have a logical connection—one being the cause of another or one giving a reason for another. For example, in verse 16 *for* shows why they cast their nets; in verse 22 Christ's teaching with authority in contrast to the scribes was the reason for the people's astonishment. The key word again is *for*.

k. *Anything strange, unusual or unexpected.* For instance, the clothing and food of John are not ordinary (v. 6).

l. *Related entities.* These can be persons, things, qualities, etc., such as Jesus, the Holy Spirit and the Father (the voice) in verses 10-11.

m. *Grammatical elements.* You must especially notice nouns, verbs, adjectives and other parts of speech in sentences that are not clear. In verse 15, *country* and *people* are subjects of the verb *went out*. In verse 10, *heavens opened* and *Spirit descending* are objects of *he saw*.

There are other features you can observe; the more you study the more you will be alert to them. Do not observe quickly or carelessly, for looking closely at the text is a basic step in good Bible study.

One way to help yourself observe carefully is to ask these six questions: What? When? Where? Who? How? Why? The answers to the first four are simply the facts in the passage. Facts ought to answer the last two also, but the last one especially may lead you to speculate, to try to imagine the reason for a saying or an act even though the reason is not given. Be careful not to read meaning into the Bible instead of getting its meaning out.

5. *Take notes.* Write down what you observe. Ideas that exist only in your mind may be muddy, but if you put them into words you can make them clear. In addition, this helps you to be accurate.

Do not try to fit things together as you first note them. Whatever you observe, write. Later as you study your comments along with the Bible passage you will see connections. You will see that some of your notes are not relevant, but others are. You can then discard the ones that do not matter.

In Mark 1 you may note a number of places where Jesus was: Judea, the Jordan River, the wilderness, Galilee. After writing them down, you can look at a map and see Jesus' movements: He came to Judea from Galilee for his baptism and temptation, then went back to Galilee to begin his ministry and call his disciples.

6. *Think and analyze.* When you have read the portion a number of times and have written down many observations, then you can meditate on them. Seek to get the meaning of the various facts.

You may think about the prophecy of the messenger preparing the Lord's way (Mk. 1:2). Who is he? John obviously. Whose way did he prepare? Christ's way. Then Christ is the Lord! How were those who repented and took John's baptism made ready for Christ's coming? What did John's message in verses 7-8 accomplish? Meditating in this way brings you the meaning of the text.

You may be struck by the fact that the temptation (v. 12) comes immediately after the heavenly word (v. 11). Does this show us something about temptation and about who are tempted? The answer should encourage us when we feel discouraged or guilty because we have been tempted.

As you meditate, questions will come to your mind to which you may or may not get immediate answers. You may ask whether verse 5 implies that all the people of Jerusalem and Judea confessed their sins and were baptized. The text does not answer this question in plain words, but it is one of the questions of interpretation you must face. Write the question down for further investigation.

Do not be disturbed if questions arise which you cannot answer. Keep them in your thought and notes. Some will be answered as you continue studying. Perhaps some may never become clear. God does not promise to answer all our questions now, but he does promise to give us the light we need.

7. *Use the principles of interpretation.* Apply them as you continue studying the passage. We will consider these principles in the following chapters.

8. *Apply the meaning of the passage.* That is, consider its relevance to your own life and to the church today. Be sure you have clearly in mind the difference between interpretation and application. When you *interpret,* you get the meaning of the passage and express this without reference to any certain person. When you *apply,* you identify how you should personally respond. The first is what God has said. The second is what God wants you to do.

"Interpretation is one, applications are many." Since this is true and since, as we have already seen, improper application can lead to bizarre, destructive behavior, we will consider this important topic at greater length in the last section of this book.

We have looked at the main steps in Bible study in a logical order. There is reason for this order and value in keeping it. Some of the steps do overlap, however. You may be reading, observing, writing and praying almost simultaneously. If you get these basic matters in your mind, you can carry them out carefully but freely. The Holy Spirit can then lead you into fruitful study.

II   General
Principles

7 Considering the Context

There are some general "laws" or "principles" that guide us in interpreting all kinds of language—narrative, sermon, poetry or whatever. We can state the first principle simply: Interpret a passage in the light of its context. Context usually means the portions surrounding the one we are studying, both before and after it. Context means what is *con* (with) the *text*.

Usually two levels of context are recognized. The near, or immediate, context is what comes just before or after the verse (say, one paragraph or perhaps two or three). The far, or remote, context may be the preceding or next chapter or some other part of the same book.

Context has many forms. Normally, a word's meaning can only be understood within a sentence or paragraph. The sentence then is the context of the word. The same is true for a phrase. A sentence by itself may even be obscure; the paragraph or section in which it is found is its context. For example, many of Jesus' parables were told on some significant occasion, and Jesus himself drew some truth from them. That setting and application are the context of the story. Poetry is a special language form. Hebrew poetry usually was written in couplets, and one half of the couplet is the context for the other, as the whole Psalm is the context for the full couplet.

It may be that some good things done by Christians have tended to make them unaware of the importance of context. One is memorizing individual verses. Of course this is good. We are to hide God's Word in our hearts. Since we cannot memorize whole books, or even chapters, easily, most of us learn verses.

But probably we have memorized some verses without realizing that they are only a part of a sentence (for example, Rom. 3:23). Surely the meaning cannot be understood without the full sentence, yet we know only the part, and that stays in our memory as something complete. Promises of Scripture are often used this way. Many times a condition to a promise is found in the verse before, yet we memorize and love the promise, ignoring the condition God has given. A glaring example of this is Isaiah 58:11: "And the Lord will guide you continually. . . ." Preceding this hopeful statement are two *if* clauses: "*If* you take away from the midst of you the yoke . . . *if* you pour yourself out for the hungry" (Is. 58:9-10).

Another good practice that sometimes has a harmful effect is using a concordance for word studies. While it is easy to look up a number of verses on *grace* or *patience*, it is hard to study each verse in its context. So we just take each verse by itself, connect it with the subject and draw out an application. This is an easy way to miss the meaning of many passages of Scripture.

Let us demonstrate the principle of context from John 9:3 in the AV. The verse contains the phrase, "neither hath this man sinned nor his parents." Does this mean that those three persons were sinless? By itself, the sentence could mean that. We know it does not, though, because the Bible clearly teaches elsewhere that no one, apart from Jesus Christ, is sinless (Rom. 3:9-10, 23). But suppose someone objects, "This verse is part of the Bible, and no matter what other verses teach, this verse says that these three people were sinless." How can we show him that he is mistaken?

By the context. Jesus was answering a question of his disciples (v. 2). Their question was not, "Have these people sinned?" Rather, they had asked, "Who sinned . . . that he was born blind?" In other words, "This man's blindness is the result of whose sin, his own or his parents'?" Jesus gave a straight answer, as in the RSV, "It [his blindness] was not that this man sinned, or his parents, but that the works of God might be made manifest in him."

So the context helps to make clear what otherwise is puzzling, what apparently contradicts the teaching of other Scripture passages.

Guidelines for Interpretation

It is not always easy to see the force of the context. Here are some guidelines to help.

1. *Think of all the possible meanings you can for the verse (or word, phrase, sentence, etc.).* You may think of one or several. Write them down. (This does not mean you should speculate or conjure up fanciful meanings.) Do you see any problem of interpretation? Write that down. It is always good to think clearly about the possible meanings of a verse and about any difficulties in it.

2. *Read the verse in the context.* You need to get familiar with the content of the section in which your verse is found, so be sure to include enough context. Do not skimp by reading only a few verses. Rather, read enough to get the progress of thought or events. The first time read it straight through, not spending time to resolve problems. Then read it again more carefully. This time note connections between words or thoughts.

3. *Study the verse more closely.* Note the connecting words (often found at the beginning of sentences), being sure to see the connection each one establishes. Examples of these words are included in the discussion of other principles of observation found in Chapter 6.

4. *Note any main words that are repeated.* Do not include common ones like *and* and *the.* Especially be alert for any word in the verse which is repeated in the verse's context. It may indicate a major theme and the relations between the parts. Note also synonyms, for example, *partake, eat, drink,* in 1 Corinthians 10:14-31.

5.*Try to write the section (your verse and its context) in your own words.* This will show if you understand the section and can express the thought clearly.

6. *Try to answer the question: What does this verse mean in its context?* If you cannot answer it, you may need to study more. There are difficult verses, however, on which even scholars do not agree, so do not be discouraged if you cannot always arrive at a clear understanding. Be willing to leave some things with God, for light he may give later.

An Example

Let us demonstrate these guidelines by looking at 1 Corinthians 10:23—" 'All things are lawful,' but not all things are helpful. 'All things are lawful,' but not all things build up." What is the possible meaning? Can *all* mean "everything with no limitation"? Then is sin—murder, adultery, selfishness, idol worship—lawful? That cannot be the meaning. But how do we know?

By reading the chapter. Verse 6 tells us "not to desire evil"; verses 7 and 14 command, "Do not be idolaters"; verse 8 says we "must not indulge in immorality." So some things are not lawful. The context shows that there are limitations. In verse 23, Paul cannot be contradicting both himself and the rest of Scripture. The context shows that one plausible interpretation is wrong. Can it also help reveal the right one?

Read chapter 10 again observantly. What is the main subject? Are any words repeated? Perhaps you notice at once that *eat* and *drink* are linked with *partake.* Note also the occasion and circumstances of each occurrence of these words. Then notice that verse 23 is surrounded by eating and drinking. Eating and drinking what? If we compare verses 19 and 28 the answer is clear—food offered in sacrifice to idols.

In verse 23 Paul is making a statement of contrast: All things are permissible but not helpful; they do not build up. In the following verses is he showing concern about something that is permissible but not helpful? Clearly, he is. Note especially in verses 32-33 his deep concern for the glory of God and for helping others. There are, then, certain permissible practices, like eating food sacrificed to idols, that have to be avoided if they hinder others and do not promote the glory of God. This is what verse 23 means.

Here are some other difficult verses to study in context: Psalms 137:4 (Are Christian hymns only for one's native land?); Daniel 6:4 (Was Daniel a sinless man?); Luke 16:15 (Does this apply to such things as secular education and the use of electricity for lighting?); Romans 14:4 (It contains a problem similar to the one in 1 Cor. 10:23.).

Context Always?

A question arises which we must face: Is context always important in Scripture? Are there some portions where it is not necessary? Say, some sayings in the book of Proverbs or some incidents in the Gospels (Lk. 13:18-24, for instance)?

The answer, I think, is that there are undoubtedly many passages where the significance of the context cannot be clearly seen. Many of the proverbs seem to be independent statements of truth without relation to the verses before and after them. (By their very nature, proverbs are short, pithy statements, complete in themselves.) Also, the authors of the narrative portions of Scripture had to select certain incidents, facts and discourses, while omitting others. So there cannot be full continuity. Often they placed together units that did not occur together. Sometimes the link is clear. Other times it is difficult to see. (In Lk. 12: 49-59, for example, several topics are mentioned that do not seem to have much relation.) We need not expect that in every case there will be a link.

Remember two things. Do not assume quickly that there is no connection if it is not apparent at once, for further study may show it. And do not try to produce a connection that is not real. We must not force the text nor read meaning into it.

Despite some exceptions, the first principle of interpretation stands: Interpret in the light of the context.

Understanding the Words

8

The second general principle of interpretation is this: Interpret according to the correct meaning of the words.

The problem, of course, is how to find the correct meaning, and for that we need to think about words in general—what they are and what they mean. Words are the building blocks of thought, speech and communication. Words put together in meaningful combinations make language, which is the primary way human beings communicate with one another. Moreover, God in the Bible used language, for the most part ordinary language, to communicate with man.

A word is a unit of language which has meaning; but because most words have more than one meaning, a word by itself rarely is clear. If I say *trunk,* you do not know whether I mean a box to put clothes in, the long nose of an elephant or the luggage space in a car. When you hear *light* by itself, you do not know whether it means the opposite of darkness, pale in color or minimal in weight. In each case you need other words to give the correct meaning.

In Revelation 5:5 the word *lion* refers to Christ, but in 1 Peter 5:8 the devil is likened to this animal. In both cases other words make the reference clear. We will also see the importance of context as we think of other facts about words.

1. *Words change their meaning over a period of time.* People use them in new ways. When the Authorized Version of the Bible was translated, the word *prevent* meant "go before." That is close to the meaning of the original language, but now, over 360 years later, its common meaning is "hinder" or "stop." The AV in 1 Thessalonians 4:15 says, "We which are alive and remain unto the coming of the Lord shall not prevent them which are asleep." True, we will not hinder them, but that is not Paul's point. In 1611 when people read "shall not prevent them," they understood it to mean "will not precede them" (as in the ASV and RSV). Verse 16 confirms this meaning: "The dead in Christ shall rise first."

If we are to interpret according to the correct meaning of the words, we must be sure (as far as we can) that what a word means to us now is what is meant when the translation we are using was made.

2. *Different words may have the same or similar meaning.* Some scholars say that the meaning of two words is never exactly the same, but sometimes it is so nearly alike that the difference does not matter. "How are you?" you ask your friend. Whether he says "I'm feeling fine" or "I'm feeling good" does not matter much. In either case you know he is in good health. If he is walking *slowly* or *leisurely,* you may have equal concern if you want him to walk *fast* or *quickly.* Many times, then, a different word does not necessarily indicate much difference in meaning. We often use synonyms simply for variety, and the Bible does this, too. We should not think that every time the Bible uses different words the meaning must be different. See the way Matthew 20:21 and Mark 10:37 use *kingdom* and *glory*; and Matthew 18:9 and Mark 9:47, *life* and *kingdom of God.*

On the other hand, sometimes we change a word in order to mean something else. We may want to use a word with a stronger or more definite meaning than one similar to it. The second word may be a synonym of the first, yet somewhat different. The biblical writers also did this.

A good example is in Galatians 6:2, 5. The AV has *burden* in both cases, but the RSV changes the second to *load*. The context shows that there is a difference: Each person should carry his own responsibility but should also help others with their problems. The different words for *prayer* in 1 Timothy 2:1 are synonyms. Do they express different kinds of prayer, or are they simply strengthening the exhortation by repetition?

3. *The Bible deals with many things that do not come into the ordinary thought of the world.* The meanings of words as people in the coffee shop use them may not be the same as when those words are used in the Bible. For instance, if you hear one man call another *a just man,* you know he probably means that the other man is fair in his dealings, that he does not cheat. This is something of what the Bible means when it says that God is just. But when the Bible speaks of a believer in Christ as *just* (Rom. 1:17 AV; RSV, *righteous*) before God, the meaning is distinct. God has declared the believer righteous in his sight. The believer has a right standing based upon the death of Christ as the atonement for his sins. The popular meaning of the word *just* does not apply.

4. *The same word may have different meanings.* Occasionally different meanings may come even in the same passage. Frequently the difference is between what are called the *literal* and *figurative* uses. Ezekiel 44:5-6 (AV) illustrates this well. In verse 5 the *house* is the literal *temple,* as the RSV translates it. But in verse 6 the nation is called the *house.* There is both a literal and a figurative sense in two successive verses. A similar example is the word *light* in Isaiah 49:6.

In the case of some words, especially what we may call "religious" words, the New Testament gives a fuller, more definite meaning than the Old. *Righteousness* is an example. The psalmist speaks of his own righteousness as his upright moral character (Ps. 18:20); but the righteousness of the full New Testament teaching is really the righteousness of

Christ that God reckons to a believer's account when he trusts Christ as his Savior (Rom. 5:17; Phil. 3:9). It is true that the Old Testament also suggests this meaning, though not as clearly as the New. (See Gen. 15:6.) *Hope* is another such word. The Old Testament believer's hope was general —the expectation that the future life would be blessed by the mercy of God. Now the Christian hope is for the second coming of Christ and the perfecting of our salvation to be like him (1 Jn. 3:2-3).

How to Study the Words

The above facts show us that if we are to understand the Bible we must understand the words, and to do this we must study them carefully. It is easy to pass over a word we do not understand, but, when we do, we cannot get the full meaning of a verse or passage. We cannot simply read a word, assume we know its meaning and keep on reading with a vague idea in our mind. We should stop to find out the meaning of the word. The Word of God is too important for us to treat in a careless way. So what are the ways to study Bible words?

1. *Look up the word in a dictionary.* A dictionary is most helpful in explaining words that have only one meaning— words like *unicorn* (Num. 23:22; Ps. 92:10 AV), *rue* (Lk. 11:42), *quaternion* (Acts 12:4 AV) and *provender* (Gen. 24: 25); and even words like *bowels* and *reins,* used in the AV (and Shakespeare) in a special figurative way for *affections* (Ps. 7:9; Phil. 1:8; 2:1; Rev. 2:23). Often the RSV or another modern version will clear up the meaning of such words.

For general words, not special ones like the above, a dictionary gives two or more—sometimes quite a few more— meanings. That is because these words are used in different ways. A dictionary rarely tells which meaning is used in the Bible. Examining several definitions helps us know the *possible* meanings of a word. It gives us an idea of what to look for, but it does not decide for us; we will have to look elsewhere to settle on the correct meaning. So for general words the dictionary is only partly helpful.

2. *Study the word in its context.* 2 Samuel 2:14 says, "And Abner said to Joab, 'Let the young men arise and *play* before us!'" It sounds like he is initiating a game, but the context shows that two rival kings and the leaders of their respective armies are involved. Verse 16 shows that the young men actually kill one another. *Play,* in this context, has a grim and ironic meaning.

"For the Lord *knows* the way of the righteous," proclaims Psalm 1:6. We might think this means only that God, since he knows all things, is aware of what righteous people do. But when we look at the near context, the second part of the verse, we learn that *know* has a stronger meaning. One way is known by God; another way perishes. The contrast shows that God's knowledge includes protection and care. Other verses also speak of God's knowledge in this way (Gen. 18:19).

To give one more example: "The *simple* believes everything" (Prov. 14:15). This may seem to be a positive statement about the good faith of a believer who is not complicated and questioning but is resting in God in simple trust. Again, the context shows the true meaning: The writer is contrasting the simple man with the prudent. The simple man (in this sense) is gullible, foolish and easily deceived. His simplicity is a weakness. Believing everything is not wisdom but folly.

The Bible is full of words whose meaning is made clear by the context. If you notice a word whose meaning is not clear, stop to consider the passage in which the word is found. Reread it if necessary. In most cases you will find some key to the meaning.

3. *Use a concordance.* I have already discussed what a concordance is and how it can help us (Chapter 5). Some words occur many times in the Bible, while others have only a few references. The ideal word study is to look at all its occur-

rences in the Bible. But smaller concordances do not list every reference, and complete ones may have too many verses for you to study. What then can you do?

Most reference Bibles have marginal references that list some other verses in which a significant word occurs. These can provide real help. And the more you study your Bible, the more you will develop your own references as you remember other passages where a particular word is found. If you have a study Bible with some margin space, you can write in such references as you find them. Since, as we have seen, words have different meanings, not every parallel passage will give additional light.

Consider Titus 3:5, where we read that "he saved us." The whole verse and the ones surrounding it convince us that this means spiritual salvation from sin. But when Luke writes, "all hope of our being saved was at last abandoned" (Acts 27:20), he was not referring to spiritual salvation but to salvation from being shipwrecked. This is so obvious it may seem a silly illustration. Yet many times in Scripture the point is not obvious, and we need to observe carefully when we find the word in other passages. What about Matthew 24:13, for instance?

You can see that words are important and must be studied carefully. For further study you could look at the following: *evil,* Jeremiah 18:11 (two occurrences; one meaning?); *continually,* Leviticus 24:2 and 1 Chronicles 16:6; *dogs,* 2 Kings 9:10 and Psalm 22:16; *body,* Ephesians 3:6 (look at all the occurrences in Ephesians); *fruit,* John 15:2, 4-5, 8, 16 (see also Gal. 5:22-23; Rom. 1:13 AV); *brethren,* Matthew 25:40; *nations,* Matthew 25:32; *crowns,* Psalm 103:4; *promise,* Ephesians 3:6 (again, see the whole epistle); and *saved through,* 1 Timothy 2:15.

9 Understanding the Grammar

The third general principle can be stated this way: Interpret according to the grammar of the sentence. What is grammar? Grammarians say it consists of two things: the form of words and the relationships of words. Both affect the meaning, but we will be concerned mainly with the second.

It is a fact that words are always used in combination, not alone, and only in this way do they have clear meaning (as we saw in the last chapter). As soon as one word is combined with others, some meaning becomes clear. Perhaps a word like *ouch* seems to mean something by itself, namely, that the speaker felt some pain. But did a bee sting him, did he sit on a thorn or did someone hit him? Other words are necessary to make the full meaning clear.

To communicate my thought to another person both of us must have the same understanding of how words are related to one another in sentences. That really means that both of us must know some grammar since grammar classifies the various ways that words are combined.

Let us see two examples of how applying grammatical principles aids interpretation. In 1 Corinthians 11:27 (AV) we read, "Wherefore whosoever shall eat this bread, and drink this cup of the Lord, unworthily...." When we ask what *unworthily* means, we have to ask whether it refers to *whosoever* or to *eat* and *drink*. That is, does it mean an unworthy *whosoever*, or *whosoever* who eats and drinks in an unworthy way? Many people think it means the first—that an unworthy person is forbidden to take communion. Then, because they themselves feel unworthy, they do not partake. When we look at the grammar, however, we see that this cannot be the meaning. The dictionary says that *unworthily* is an adverb, and the grammar books tell us that adverbs modify verbs, not nouns. So *unworthily* refers to the eating and drinking, not to the person.

Versions like the RSV and others translate *unworthily* with the phrase *in an unworthy manner*. No one should hesitate to take part in the communion because he is unworthy. (If he is deliberately holding sin in his life, that is another matter.) We are all unworthy. It is because of Christ's death and his worthiness, which is ours as believers, that we may and should take part. But we may partake unworthily: We may not have proper reverence or spiritual discernment; we may not have the right concern for others; we may be occupied with physical food. It is to such evils that the verse refers. We know this is so because of the grammar, because we recognize that one important word is an adverb rather than an adjective.

Or consider John 21:15. Jesus asked Peter, "Simon, son of John, do you love me more than *these*?" Immediately we think, more than whom or what? The dictionary tells us that *these* is a demonstrative pronoun, the plural of *this*. When we look up *this* we learn that it is a demonstrative pronoun or adjective "denoting a person or thing near, topical, just mentioned or about to be mentioned." We note that it may refer to a person or thing and to one which is in the near context. Were there persons near when Jesus spoke to Peter? Yes, some of the disciples. Were there things near? Yes, some fish just caught. So knowing the grammar helps us to see two possible meanings for *these*. We have to use other principles to determine which of the two is right. The context (v. 1) tells us that Peter had turned back to fishing, even though Jesus had called him from that. So he may have loved the fish (his occupation) more than Jesus. Peter himself had earlier said, in effect, that he loved Jesus more than the other disciples did (Mt. 26:33), so perhaps Jesus was challenging him about that boast.

Grammar may not always show us the actual meaning, but it will show us possible meanings. We cannot accept any meaning that does violence to it. Thus grammar is important in understanding the Bible. This is not strange. Essentially it means that we understand the Bible according to the normal laws of human language.

Know the Elements of Grammar

If we are to interpret the Bible according to grammar, we must know something about grammar. It would be good for you to refresh your knowledge by getting a grammar book and reading it. Be sure you understand the parts of speech: noun, verb, pronoun, adjective, adverb, preposition, conjunction and interjection. The important thing is the way each of these relates to other words in a sentence and how this relationship affects meaning. You do not need to know all the fine points, but you should understand the basic ones.

An ordinary English sentence tells us something about the subject. The subject is something, does something or has something done to it: Johnny is a boy. He steals apples and is punished. Usually, the subject is put first. *God is love* tells us something about God. So also, *the Lord is blessed.* Sometimes, however, the word order is changed, especially in poetry. The Psalms often say "Blessed be the Lord." This still tells us something about the Lord. The meaning has not changed, except that there may now be a stronger emphasis on the word *blessed.*

We must be careful, though, at this point. If we say,

"Love is God," we have used the same words as when we say "God is love," but the meaning has changed. Now we are saying something about love. Some people say there is no difference in the two sentences, but that destroys the biblical teaching about God. He is not identical with love. A mother's love is not the same as God. We must observe Bible sentences carefully, noting when and how the word order affects the meaning.

Verbs and Their Tenses

Verbs, the "action words" of sentences, are important for understanding any language, including the Bible's. One of the things we need to consider is their *tense,* or *time.* A verb usually refers to either past, present or future time: "I ate, I eat, I will eat." But because it is not that simple, let us look more closely.

1. *Past tense.* A past tense may show that something happened once in the past. Romans 7:9, "Sin revived and I died." It may also show something that happened many times, something repeated or habitual. 1 Corinthians 13: 11, "I spoke ... I thought ... I reasoned like a child."

2. *Present tense.* The present tense may show a universal truth, one not limited to any particular time. John 4:24, "God is Spirit." The point is not that God is Spirit just now or that he goes on being Spirit, but that this is his nature. The present may also express what is permanently true, continuous or habitual. Luke 12:54, "When you see a cloud ... you say." This is true over and over. Matthew 23:13, "You neither enter yourselves, nor ..." shows a continued attitude and practice. The present can even express the future, usually what will happen very soon. Matthew 26:2, "The Passover is coming."

3. *Future tense.* The future tense normally tells what will happen in the future. John 14:3, "I will come." But it may also imply a command. Matthew 5:21 (quoting the Old Testament), "You shall not kill." Though the form is future, the

meaning is timeless.

A special problem with tenses comes in the prophetic portions of Scripture, especially in the Old Testament. (See also Chapter 19, No. 4.) Much of the prophecy relating to the future is expressed by verbs in the future tense—but not all. Sometimes the past may be used. Isaiah 53 is mostly in the past tense, but it refers to Christ's future work. Matthew 8:16-17 shows that Isaiah 53:4, "surely he has borne our griefs," was fulfilled hundreds of years after the prophecy was given. In prophecy the present tense may also be used for the future. Psalm 22 is largely in the present tense, though it prophesies Christ's death. (Compare v. 18 with Jn. 19:23-24.)

Does this make the Bible's use of tenses confusing? Does it mean there is no real meaning in them or that the meaning is too difficult for us to find? Not at all. We have been thinking about the possible meanings of the tenses. When we know the possible, we are helped toward finding out the actual. So we study a particular passage, keeping in mind what the tenses may possibly mean. Then we look at the context and at other Scripture, and usually we can tell the actual meaning. There are problems, of course; we must be prepared for serious, prayerful study.

Sometimes the tense may affect the meaning in a way that we cannot easily see. For example, 1 John 3 seems to contain a significant problem of interpretation. Verses 6 and 9 contain these statements, "No one who sins has either seen him or known him. . . . No one born of God commits sin." Are these verses to be understood in an absolute way? Do they say that no true Christian ever commits a sin? Some Christians believe this is the meaning, but most Bible students do not, because such a meaning contradicts other biblical statements. These verses seem to say this, however, so we must look at them carefully.

We note that the tense of *sins* and *commits* is present, and we remember that a present tense can have different meanings. We look further at the epistle and notice some other points: (1) John is writing to believers (2:11-14); (2) he definitely suggests the possibility of their sinning (2:1, 15; 3:11-12); and (3) in that possibility he even includes himself (1:8; 3:16-18). So we ask, if 3:6-9 really means that to sin, even to commit one sin, shows that a person is not a Christian, then why say to Christians, "I am writing this to you so that you may not sin" (2:1) and "If we say we have no sin, we deceive ourselves" (1:8)?

What else could 3:6-9 mean? The present tense can mean that which is continuous or habitual. Would that be a reasonable interpretation? We continue to read 1 John carefully and note that he presents strongly some opposite alternatives: light and darkness, truth and error, life and death, righteousness and sin. Each of these is presented absolutely, as though it is all this or all that; all light or all darkness, all righteousness or all sin. We know, however, and the Word of God recognizes, that our experience is not absolute. John himself recognizes it. Therefore, we understand that John is presenting in this strong language a truth that is found throughout the Bible: The person who knows God is to live a life marked by holiness and righteousness; he cannot go on habitually sinning. This is confirmed by some of the other versions, which would be worth checking to clarify the point.

Pronouns, Genitives and Conjunctions

Pronouns are simple words, it seems, but we need to watch them carefully. A pronoun stands for a noun. In the sentence "Jesus came to Bethany and on the next day he entered Jerusalem" the pronoun *he* stands for Jesus. Sometimes there is no problem seeing what noun the pronoun refers to. "Jack went out and he met Tom." *He* can refer only to Jack. But what about this one: "Jack went to Tom and he gave him a book"? Can we be certain who gave the book to whom? If the sentence is in a context, probably we would know because of what else is said.

Usually in English, and in the Bible as well, a pronoun refers to the nearest noun; but this is not always true. Let us look at some verses.

Acts 7:59: "As they were stoning Stephen, he prayed." No problem there.

Luke 11:37: "While he was speaking, a Pharisee asked him to dine with him; so he went in and sat at table." Who went in? Jesus, obviously, even though *Pharisee* is the noun nearest the pronoun. In the context the meaning is clear. (See also 2 Chron. 24:24; Jn. 13:1, 3; 11:3.)

Study Ephesians 1:3-11 in the RSV. Here the meaning of the pronouns is not so clear. Sometimes *he* refers to God the Father and sometimes to Christ. We must look closely to notice where the meaning changes.

Isaiah 37:36 (AV): "Then the angel of the Lord went forth, and smote in the camp of the Assyrians a hundred and four-score and five thousand: and when they arose early in the morning, behold, they were all dead corpses." This verse sounds funny because it sounds as though the dead men rose. The confusion is caused by using *they* twice. The RSV makes the sense clear by changing the words slightly: "when men arose early in the morning, behold, these were all dead bodies."

You can also study Deuteronomy 32:15-16 to see whether *you, he* and *they* are three groups or one. And Mark 5:18— Who would be with whom?

Pronouns affect the meaning very much. At times, especially in the prophetic books of the Old Testament, close study is needed to see the referents of pronouns. Try Exodus 1:12 (AV); Isaiah 10:27 (*his,* cf. v. 26); and Isaiah 33:5-6 (*he* and *his*).

Two other combinations of words we need to discuss are called the *objective* and *subjective genitive*. Each begins with a noun that has some verbal idea in it, like *love, fear* or *call*. A preposition joins that noun with another in what is called *a genitive construction,* such as *the love of God.* Now the question comes: Is God loving or being loved? Is he the subject or object of the verbal idea (love)? Both meanings are possible, but not both at once. We must interpret to decide which is correct in a given passage. If God is the lover, this is a subjective genitive; if the beloved, then an objective genitive.

For example, 2 Corinthians 5:14, "the love of Christ controls us." Is it Christ's love for us (he is the subject) or our love for him (he is the object)? We would have to go to the context, possibly to some parallel passages, to get an answer. And there may be passages where we are not able to decide for certain which is meant. Some other verses with this construction are Genesis 18:20 (AV); John 5:42; and 1 Timothy 4:1.

Conjunctions, the main connecting words in sentences, are also important to meaning. Think of a simple sentence: "I eat vegetables and I am strong." Now think of the sentence with other connecting words in place of *and.* For example, "I eat vegetables because I am strong." Then, "I eat vegetables when I am strong." Substitute in turn *yet, therefore* and *although.* Think about how the meaning changes in each sentence. The conjunction *for* is found in these three verses: Luke 12:15, 23 and 32. It is not hard to see how this connective word links the commands not to be greedy, to worry or to fear to a strong reason for obeying them.

There are other grammatical elements you should know. For lack of space, we will not consider them here, but if you want to know your Bible thoroughly, you will want to familiarize yourself with them. A grammar book can have a spiritual ministry!

Some More Guidelines
Here are four more guidelines to help you apply the principles of grammar:

1. *Where the meaning of a verse or passage is not clear, identify the key word and label it grammatically, that is, what part of speech it is, how it is related to other words, etc.* Check with a dictionary and grammar book if necessary.

2. *Study the relation of this word to others around it.*

3. *Note the possible meanings it may give the section.*

4. *If there is more than one possible meaning, consider other principles, especially context.*

Let us try this on a passage: John 1:41, "he first found his brother Simon, and said to him." We do not need to examine all the words of the verse carefully because there is not much problem in understanding them. One word, though, does give some difficulty, the word *first*. It is an easy word, but the difficulty is seeing how it relates to the sentence. When we hear the word *first,* we think of a sequence; we expect a *second,* perhaps a *third* or more. So here there must be something following the first thing mentioned. What is it?

A dictionary tells us that *first* can be an adjective (as when we say, "the first year") or an adverb (meaning "before anything else"). As an adjective in John 1:41 it would mean that *Andrew* was first in some sense. Perhaps he was the first person to find his brother and then a friend found his brother afterward. Each man did it but Andrew was first. As an adverb *first* would mean that Andrew *did* something first, before doing something else. First he found his brother; afterward he found some others.

Do each of these meanings make sense? If so, then both are possible interpretations. Which is likely right? Are there any principles to guide us? Is there anything in the context that will help us decide? Nothing that is definitive, as far as I see. Try parallel passages. Look up other places where Andrew is mentioned in the New Testament: Mark 13:3; John 6:8; 12:22; and Acts 1:13. What is prominent among the things that Andrew did? Is it true then that after bringing his brother to Jesus he brought others also? Can this be a key to our verse?

You will find many problems in the grammar of Bible passages. As you study them, you will grow in understanding God's Word. For further study you may see:

Deuteronomy 15:6: "You shall not borrow"—promise or command?

Psalm 14:1: To what does the pronoun *they* (plural!) refer?

Psalm 37:1: "Fret not yourself." Who is the subject of the verb? What is the significance of this?

Proverbs 5:21: Read both the AV and RSV and identify the referents of *he* and *his*.

Luke 24:48: "You are witnesses of these things." What is the force of *these*?

Romans 8:24: Which is better, *by hope* (AV) or *in this hope* (RSV)? What does it mean?

2 Corinthians 5:19: "God was in Christ reconciling the world to himself." To what is *in Christ* connected? Does it mean simply that God was in Christ, thus implying his divine nature? Or is it that God was reconciling through Christ, that is, that Christ was the one through whom God did the reconciling? Both meanings are possible grammatically.

10 Grasping the Author's Intention

The fourth general principle covers two things: Interpret according to the author's purpose and plan. These two are so closely related that, while we must see the difference between them, we can consider them together.

The *purpose* of the author is the object he has in mind for writing. When John writes in 1 John 5:13, "I write this to you . . . *that* you may know that you have eternal life," he plainly states his purpose. The *plan* of the author is the way he structures the writing in order to carry out his purpose. Ephesians, for instance, has a recognizable pattern: The first three chapters give the calling of the Christian and the last three discuss his behavior. We learn this partly from the *therefore* at the beginning of chapter 4.

In the above examples the purpose and plan are easy to see, but not always are they so clear. In fact in most of the books of the Bible the purpose is not stated, and in the majority of those it is difficult to learn. The plan of a book is usually more evident than the purpose. Since we cannot apply the fourth principle unless we can learn the author's purpose and plan, and since discovering them is often difficult, this principle is harder to use than some others and therefore we may not use it as much. But it is important, so we shall consider some examples of how to apply it.

The Author's Purpose

John states in 20:31 his purpose for writing his Gospel: "But these [signs] are written that you may believe that Jesus is the Christ, the Son of God, and that believing you may have life in his name." John described Jesus' miracles so that people would come to believe on Jesus as the Son of God (his person) and through that faith receive eternal life (salvation). Three great realities are here: the person of Christ, faith and life. John says he wrote about the signs so that people will experience these realities.

It follows, then, that each miracle will probably reveal something of the person of Christ and of the meaning of faith and life. We should keep this in mind in seeking to understand the meaning of each miracle. We can take, for example, Jesus' first sign, recorded in John 2:1-11. What does it reveal about the person of Christ? Certainly that he is the Creator, the sovereign of the physical creation. The disciples also recognized that his miraculous work "manifested his glory," as verse 11 suggests.

The sign also reveals something about spiritual life. Human existence is marked by failure, as is suggested by the wine failing. But Christ gives abundant life, with no shortage and better quality ("the good wine"). This life is marked by sufficiency and satisfaction.

There is teaching about faith here, too. Mary's trust, her complete confidence in Christ, is shown in verse 5: "Do whatever he tells you." Faith leads to obedient action, and the servants obeyed when Jesus commanded them. Jesus worked through that confidence and obedience, and the people experienced a miracle. The disciples experienced it as well and "believed in him" (v. 11). Knowing John's purpose, then, helps us see the spiritual thrust of the miracles.

The Author's Plan

An example of interpreting in the light of the author's plan can be found in the book of Genesis. Reading Genesis carefully one notices the repetition of the phrase *These are the generations of* (Gen. 2:4; 5:1; 6:9; 10:1; 11:10, 27; 25:12, 19; 36:1, 9; 37:2—the RSV translates a few of these slightly differently). So many occurrences of the phrase cannot be accidental. What is the significance, and how will this help us understand the book? To see the force of the phrase in each reference, make a table with columns, listing the relevant facts connected with each occurrence: person mentioned, content of section (that is, genealogy, personal story, etc.), length of section.

As you study, various facts will come to light. For example, Genesis has two parts: the first, up to Abraham; the second, Abraham and the patriarchs that follow him. The first part gives mainly genealogies, the second tells stories of individuals. The whole book shows God's plan working out through the godly "seed" or line. God's personal concern for Ishmael and Esau is revealed, but also the fact that they are not in the line of his purpose. Abraham and Jacob are given much space, despite their serious weaknesses, because they were chosen by God for his purpose.

So where the purpose and/or plan of a book can be known, we are to interpret the book and various passages in their light. The purpose of John's Gospel and the plan of Genesis are good examples of this.

Finding Purpose and Plan
The main question is whether we can know the author's purpose and plan. Here are some suggestions for finding it:

1. *Note whether the purpose is stated or not.* If not, are there any hints or indications of it? Nowhere in his two letters to the Corinthians does Paul clearly state his purpose, but we can discover by comparing passages like 1 Corinthians 1:11; 3:4; 4:6; 5—6; 7:1, 18; 8:1; 12:1; 16:1; 2 Corinthians 2:3-4; 7:5-8; 10—13. From these passages we learn that some Christians related to Chloe had brought Paul bad news about the Corinthian church. There were factions,

lawsuits, immorality and disorder at the communion service. Some in the church were rejecting Paul's authority because some other teachers spoke more eloquently. Then the Corinthians wrote Paul a letter, asking him certain questions. He replied (1 Corinthians), expressing himself so strongly that he feared there might be hurt feelings. When Titus brought him word that the Corinthians had responded well, he wrote again (2 Corinthians), telling of his thanksgiving to God but also warning them against certain false apostles. From these facts we can deduce his purpose for writing each letter.

Be careful, however, about judging only from hints. They should be clear indicators. It is not good to make guesses from vague phrases. We do not have to know the particular purpose of each book in order to understand it, but if the purpose is clear this aids our comprehension.

2. *Personal references to the readers usually indicate a book's purpose.* Also, themes or subjects that are repeated or emphasized may suggest it. Surely Matthew wrote his Gospel partly at least to set forth the truth of the kingdom of heaven, since he refers to it so many times.

3. *Look for the structure of the book.* There may be clear division points, such as 12:1 in Romans or 4:1 in Ephesians. There may be repeated words or phrases, as in Genesis. But be careful here too. The phrase *heavenly places* or *heavenlies* occurs five times in Ephesians but does not indicate the book's divisions. Again, do not merely speculate.

4. *When the purpose and/or plan is clear, then study each portion of the book with that in mind, being sure that your interpretation squares with it.*

Let us consider one other passage with the above suggestions in mind. Philippians 2:1-8 is a passage that shows the purpose of an author. The phrases *the same mind, the same love, full accord* and *one mind* show that Paul is bothered about the quality of fellowship of the Philippian Christians. So in verses 5-8 he reminds them of Christ's example.

Christ had a certain mind, so he acted in certain ways. He did not grasp after equality with God (v. 6); he emptied himself (v. 7); and he humbled himself even to the shameful criminal's death of the cross (v. 8). So Christ's death is given as an example of humility. The point here is not that his death shows God's love or atones for our sins, as is taught in many other passages. The purpose of the author guides his emphasis in each passage.

Here are some other passages to which you can apply the fourth general principle of interpretation:

Proverbs 1:1-6: How does the purpose stated here affect the meaning of other passages?

In Ecclesiastes: The phrase *under the sun* may be the key to this book. Does knowing this help with puzzling verses like 2:17, 20, 24; 9:4?

Luke 1:1-4: Answer the same question as in Proverbs.

In Galatians 1: Consider Paul's purpose in light of his repeated use of the word *gospel* and his abrupt beginning (without thanksgiving).

In Colossians: Study 2:4, 8, 16, 20-22 for suggestions regarding Paul's purpose.

11

Studying the Background

The fifth general principle is: Interpret in the light of the historical, geographical and cultural background, as far as that can be known.

Events in the Bible took place at certain times in history. They shared the culture of the people living then, mainly the Jews. The New Testament relates to the culture of Palestine in the first century A.D. and to the history of that time and before. We can easily misunderstand the New Testament if we interpret it according to our own culture.

We must keep in mind that the same act, statement or incident may well mean different things in different cultures. For example, in England if a man speaks of a woman as *homely,* he is complimenting her, for there the word means "home-loving" and "unpretentious." But in America *homely* insults a woman because it means "ugly." In some parts of India you insult a man when you call him an *owl* or *a son of an owl,* while in America this is praise. To the Indian it means stupidity, but to the American, wisdom!

An expression or idiom that has meaning in one culture or at one time in history may have *no* meaning in another. Because meanings change, we need to understand biblical expressions in their cultural context. In 2 Kings 2:9 Elisha asks Elijah that he might receive *a double portion* of Elijah's spirit. In our culture we might think that means he wanted twice as much of the spirit (perhaps the Holy Spirit) that Elijah had. But in the light of the cultural background of these two men (especially Deut. 21:17) it seems clear that Elisha was asking for the inheritance of the first-born: He wanted to be Elijah's heir.

So remember, the first and primary meaning of a passage is what it meant in its historical and cultural context—that is, what it should have meant to the people living then. As best we can, we must understand that meaning. It is primary.

A good example of this is Luke 9:23, one of the verses in which Jesus states that anyone who wants to follow him must "take up his cross daily." We talk about taking up our cross as putting up with difficulties, hardships or trying persons. In Jesus' day, however, the one who took up his cross was a criminal on the way to execution. He took up the cross to go to death. So the people of his day understood Jesus' words in that sense. They knew that Jesus was talking about death (physical or spiritual), not some hardship. Other passages in the Gospels, especially those telling about Jesus' own death, bring out this meaning clearly. We must interpret only with that meaning.

We recognize that we may not be able to find out the original meaning of all passages. There are some references, fortunately not a large number, such as Exodus 28:30—"Urim and Thummin"—and 1 Corinthians 15:29—"baptized on behalf of the dead"—where no Bible scholar can say precisely what the original meaning was. For the most part, however, by using the principles of interpretation we can know the original meaning and interpret accordingly.

We also recognize that there may be a fuller meaning in earlier parts of the Bible than the people of that time could have understood. When God first spoke the promise of Christ's coming (Gen. 3:15), no one could have understood the full significance of the "seed's" heel and the "serpent's" head being bruised. When Jesus called Zaccheus a *son of Abraham* (Lk. 19:9), the hearers could hardly have realized the full meaning as indicated in Galatians 3:7, 29. So there may have been fuller meaning revealed later, but the original meaning is still primary.

In 1 Samuel 12:17 is an example of how knowing the cultural background aids understanding. Samuel says he will call upon the Lord to send rain at the time of the wheat harvest. Normally there was no rain from April to October, and the wheat harvest went on from mid-April to mid-May. This was an evidence, therefore, of God's power, which showed the people that Samuel was speaking from the Lord.

In Mark 11:12-14 (also Mt. 21:18-19) is the record of Christ's cursing the fig tree. Mark 11:13 seems to say that Christ cursed the tree because there were no figs on it even though it was not the fig season, and that seems unfair. But even out of season good fig trees have some figs, so it was reasonable to expect to find at least a few. Their absence showed that the tree was not fruitful.

It is easy to see that the background is important in the interpretation of Scripture. The background includes different elements:

1. *Historical elements.*

Daniel 5:7, 16: Daniel was made the third ruler because Belshazzar and his father were then ruling together; there were two rulers already.

Matthew 2:22: History tells us that Archelaus was a greater threat to Jesus' life than his father was.

2. *Geographical elements.*

John 4:4: Jesus had to pass through Samaria because that province was between Judea and Galilee.

Joel 2:23: There were two main rainy seasons, the autumn or early rain at the time of sowing crops and the spring or latter rain to mature the harvest.

3. *Cultural elements (social, religious or material).*

Luke 9:59: To bury his father was a sacred responsibility for the oldest son and might involve years of waiting if the father were not already dead.

John 13:3-5: Washing the feet of guests was the duty of a servant, and none of the disciples was willing, apparently, to do this service.

Learning the Background

To interpret in the light of the background we have to find out that background. How do we acquire that knowledge? We can get much valuable material from the works of Bible scholars—Bible dictionaries, geographies, commentaries, etc. If you can obtain any of these, use them. If you cannot remember that you can find all the *essential* background information in the Bible itself. A basic principle we have already noticed is that the Bible is its own best interpreter. The Bible gives background information for most obscure passages.

How can you learn this information? Here are some steps to follow:

1. *Learn the Bible.* Read, read, read it. The more you are familiar with the whole Bible, the more you will have background knowledge to help you in interpretation. Read the historical books. The Old Testament history is background for both the Old and New Testaments. The Pentateuch contains much cultural background for the rest of the Bible, and especially for the New Testament. Later passages may also shed light on earlier ones. By thoughtful and repeated reading you will acquire knowledge of the times and culture of Bible people.

2. *Make notes as you read.* Write down details about Bible characters, customs, features of the land. Note unusual things, strange words, etc. Then look them up and write down their meaning. Include the Bible reference of any fact you record. This will help you to find it later and check for accuracy. Taking notes regularly is a valuable aid for

understanding the Bible. It helps your memory and increases your store of usable knowledge.

3. *If you have a Bible with marginal references, use them.* Some editions of the AV and RSV have a good system of references. Often New Testament verses have a reference to the Old Testament. By John 3:14, which speaks of Moses lifting up the serpent, there will be a reference to Numbers 21:9. Those already in your Bible are not complete, however, so make your own references as you study. When one verse reminds you of another, note the other verse in the margin.

4. *Use the maps in your Bible to locate geographical points.* For example, if as you read Joshua you look up the places mentioned in it, you will understand the plan of the conquest. Find Gibeon in relation to Joshua's location in chapter 9.

5. *If other books are available, use them, too.* The first is a dictionary. Many cultural items are explained in the definitions of words. We have already considered a number of words that have to do with culture; other examples are *aloes, cassia, nitre, shittim, brimstone, psaltery* and *timbrel.* Bible dictionaries and commentaries, of course, explain many cultural items, since these items affect interpretation.

Guidelines for Interpretation

Once you have information about the background of a passage, you are ready to think about the interpretation. For this, these three simple guidelines are helpful:

1. *Consider carefully any points that are unknown or confusing in the passage and note how a knowledge of the background helps in understanding them.*

2. *Determine what the passage must have meant to the people in that setting.*

3. *Seek to understand what meaning is relevant for us today in our culture and make an appropriate application.*

Let us use as an example Judges 13:3-5, where the angel

of the Lord said to Manoah's wife that the son she was to bear would be "a Nazarite to God from birth." What did the angel mean by *Nazarite*? A Bible with references doubtlessly will refer to Numbers 6. If you do not have a reference Bible, you can get help from a Bible dictionary, which will briefly define the word and refer you to Numbers 6 for the full explanation. In Numbers we learn that a Nazarite is one who makes a special vow of separation or dedication to the Lord. In fulfilling that vow he is to abstain from things of common life in three areas: from drinking wine or eating anything related to the grape, from cutting his hair and from contact with a dead person.

The significance of this clearly seems to be that when a person wished to be dedicated to the Lord for a particular purpose or work, and took a vow to that effect, then he was to separate himself from certain activities which were otherwise quite permissible. Grapes were a main crop in Palestine, a basic source of food and drink for the Israelites. Cutting the hair seems to have been normal for men since not cutting is made a mark of separation. Corpses had to be touched in preparation for burial, and this was a normal duty, though Numbers 19 indicates that one doing it had to be purified from uncleanness afterward and Leviticus 21 teaches that the priests were not to do it except for certain near relatives. But the Nazarite was to abstain completely. No reason is stated for making these particular prohibitions rather than others, and certainly the Nazarite was free to engage in most normal occupations.

So the teaching for the people then was that when a person wished to dedicate himself in a special way to the Lord he made a vow, and in fulfilling that vow he abstained from certain normal activities and responsibilities. This was the condition put upon the boy Samson from his birth. Obviously, then, it must have been the parents who made the vow on his behalf.

If we wish to apply this to ourselves, we do not have plain

instructions in the New Testament about how to do so. In fact, no mention of the Nazarite is made there. So we have to apply the principle as given in the Old Testament. A Christian today may wish to dedicate himself in a special way or for a special purpose to the Lord. So he can make a vow and while fulfilling it separate himself from certain activities. The activities mentioned in Numbers 6 probably will not be relevant, but he can seek God's guidance about the mark of his separation. He may want to take counsel from spiritual leaders in the matter. However, there is no legal requirement for him in such a case.

This is a good approach to use in seeking to interpret in the light of the background. Many passages will pose bigger problems, either in learning the background, understanding the meaning for that time or making a relevant application. But the more you study such passages, and the whole Bible, the more light will come: Your understanding of God's Word will grow.

For further study: 1 Kings 13 (significance of Bethel in relation to Judah); 2 Kings 3:11 (Elisha poured water); 2 Kings 4:1-7 (the woman's situation); Matthew 8:4 (showing to the priest); Acts 15:20, 29 (these necessary things—to what extent are they fundamental or to what extent related to Jewish scruples?); 1 Corinthians 11:1-16 (is there a cultural factor in the woman's veil?); 2 Timothy 1:8 (his prisoner).

12 Interpreting Scripture by Scripture

This is the sixth principle: Interpret each passage in the light of the Bible's teaching as a whole. It is another way of saying, "Interpret Scripture by Scripture." If you follow the other principles as best you can but the resulting interpretation contradicts other biblical teaching, your interpretation is questionable. The Bible does not contradict itself. The Bible is essentially one revelation, giving one message about God.

We have already seen that a verse or passage must be studied in its context—the verses, paragraphs and even chapters that surround it. The implication of this sixth principle is that the whole Bible is the ultimate context of a passage. The message of the Bible on a particular subject can be found only by studying all the passages relating to it. If we study only some of the passages, we may fail to understand the Bible's teaching.

Suppose you are going through a jungle. Cutting across your path is a river that is difficult to cross. If you know nothing about the general area, you will try to cross the river, but if you know that a quarter of a mile to the right the river makes a bend and reverses its direction, you will simply walk around the bend. Some general knowledge will save you from great difficulty, even danger. There is great value in the overall view.

Knowing the whole Bible will keep us from concluding that we know what a verse means while actually misunderstanding what the Bible teaches. For example, we may read Ephesians 3:14 where Paul says, "For this reason I bow my knees before the Father." We may then conclude that since Paul knelt for his prayer, the Bible teaches that we also should kneel when we pray. This would be to ignore passages that show that both standing and lying prostrate are legitimate postures for prayer as well as passages that suggest that the attitude of the heart rather than the position of the body is what pleases God.

Heresies and false doctrines seem to have biblical authority because those who teach them use only certain passages and ignore others. We can be kept from believing wrong doctrine by checking our understanding of a verse by the message of the whole Bible. We should maintain a humble attitude and not be quick to form final or dogmatic conclusions about the meaning of one verse until we have considered it in the light of the whole Word of God.

Some Bible students consider only one section when interpreting or forming a doctrine. For example, they take the restrictions on food given in the Old Testament and use them as the basis for Christian conduct today. Or they reflect on God's promises in the Old Testament to bless those who keep his law and, without considering the New Testament teaching about God's way of justification, conclude that people in the Old Testament period could be righteous in God's sight by obedience to the law.

The doctrine of the Sabbath is one for which this principle is vital. In the Old Testament the teaching of the Sabbath as the seventh day of rest is quite clear, but to get the full biblical teaching, and especially the meaning of the doctrine for today, we must consider both Testaments together, including the relation of the old and new covenants, the meaning of Christ's resurrection and the practice of the early church.

On the other hand, some take the New Testament alone and ignore the Old. Though they may read the Old Testament to understand the New, they consider that the New Testament is sufficient for learning all the truth Christians need to know. We will consider in Chapter 21 the relation of the Old and New Testaments, so we will simply note here that *all* of the Bible is God's revelation, and each part is to be understood in the light of the whole.

Still another way of ignoring this principle is by taking some truth from the Gospels or Acts without considering the teaching of the Epistles along with it. Some Christians derive their doctrine of the baptism of the Holy Spirit almost entirely from the Acts. The baptism of the Spirit is an important truth; it can be understood clearly only by considering the teaching of the whole New Testament.

Parallel Passages

One way to get the teaching of the whole Bible is to study what are called *parallel passages*: verses in different parts of the Bible that discuss the same thing. For instance, we find some of the sayings of Jesus and some incidents recorded in two or more of the Gospels. The history in Samuel and Kings is parallel to Chronicles, in part. Not quite so exactly, but still parallel, are portions of Ephesians and Colossians, of Romans and Galatians.

In considering parallel passages, keep these guidelines in mind:

1. *Be sure the parallel is a true one.* Though the same word occurs in two verses, there may be no parallel. (See *fall* in Judg. 18:1 and 20:44.) There must be a clear similarity of thought.

2. *Note carefully both differences and similarities.* Write them down, so you see them clearly. Consider how each difference affects the meaning. Study each verse in its context.

In Matthew 10:34 Jesus says, "I have not come to bring

peace, but a sword." Is this literal? When we read the context, we see mention of *foes* (v. 36), and that sounds like fighting.

Luke 12:51 is a parallel passage. The sentence is almost the same, but not quite. *Sword* is changed to *division*. Both passages mention a household and divided families, with differing details. So the thought is the same, for there is a similar context. A sword is symbolic of fighting and therefore means division. We can, therefore, question whether the verse in Matthew means actually using a sword. When we read on to Matthew 10:37-38, we see that the issue being faced is who is first. If a man puts Christ first in his life, there will often be division between him and his family.

Parallel passages do not always exist, so the above guidelines are not as important as the context principle, but it would be worthwhile for you to study some more examples: (1) Compare 1 Corinthians 8:6 and Colossians 1:16. Some understand Colossians 1:16 to refer to the new, spiritual creation. (2) One person linked Isaiah 9:6-7 with 1 Samuel 17:40. Note the *five* in each (though the RSV punctuates to show four names instead of five). Is there any connection?

Knowing the Whole Bible

The practical question we face is, How can we acquire a knowledge of the whole Bible? Here are some guidelines:

1. *Read the Bible extensively.* In addition to the shorter reading you do in your quiet time, have a plan for reading the Bible through in a regular period. Once a year may be all you can manage, and even that will take time and effort. A simple rule for a yearly reading is three chapters each day and five on Sunday. Since chapters are longer or shorter, this does not give an equal amount for each day, so you may wish to choose another plan from the many available. By observing carefully and making notes, you will be able to remember passages and gradually learn to compare Scrip-

ture with Scripture. Without this work your progress in learning the Bible will be much slower.

2. *Study the Bible regularly.* Reading alone is not sufficient. You should combine reading and study by taking sufficient time each day for it. Try to have a plan for studying the Bible book-by-book till you have completed it. *This Morning with God* and *Search the Scriptures* (both published by Inter-Varsity Press) are two very good plans for such study. The former will take you through the Bible in just over four years, the latter in three years, which means that the daily portion for study is not too long for busy people.

Perhaps you are now feeling discouraged, thinking you can never know the whole Bible, at least not for many years. In one sense this is true. No one can know the Bible fully, even after decades of study. Reading and studying regularly, systematically and prayerfully, however, will insure that your knowledge of the Word of God is continually growing.

III

Special Principles

13

Figures
of
Speech

Besides the general principles that guide us in interpreting all language, special types of language require special principles. In this section we look at some special types of language and the principles that help us understand them. First, we will consider figures of speech.

A *figure of speech* is a word or phrase that is used to communicate something other than its literal, natural meaning. We all use such expressions frequently. "That argument doesn't hold water," we say, though an argument has nothing to do with literal water. This sentence means that like a canteen with holes in it the argument is useless. We are told to "stand up for the Word of God." Are we to stand up physically when someone asks us if we believe in the Bible? No, this means we should speak out, act and in every way make our convictions clear. If I say "I was tickled to death," that does not make you feel sorry for me because you know I was not tortured but only extremely amused.

These figures that people use in ordinary speech are not true in their literal sense, but they are true. They simply express truth in a different way—a more vivid and interesting way. We take in the meaning without stopping to think that the expression is a figure or to imagine what it would mean literally; our minds translate it automatically.

It is important, however, to recognize the figures of speech in the Bible. Sometimes it does not matter much whether a statement is literal or figurative. At other times it matters a great deal. Martin Luther and Ulrich Zwingli, two leaders of the Reformation, were once discussing the Scriptures. They talked about the communion service and particularly the words of Christ *This is my body*. The Roman Catholic Church taught that this statement is literal, that the bread and wine actually become the physical flesh and blood of Christ. Luther, too, believed it to be literal, though he could not go as far as the Catholic view. Zwingli, however, insisted that it is a metaphor, that the bread and wine *represent* the body and blood of Christ and that Christ is present spiritually but not physically in the communion. The two leaders could not agree, and the Reformation churches were split over this matter. So whether a certain word or phrase is literal or figurative is sometimes a significant question.

Figures of Comparison

The Scripture uses a number of different figures of speech. There are names commonly used for them, and it is good to know these technical terms. We will first consider the two figures of speech that show comparison.

1. *Metaphor*. A metaphor is an implied (rather than actually stated) comparison between two things that are basically unlike. If you compare a dog and a jackal, you do not have a metaphor because the two animals are alike; but you can make a metaphor by comparing a man and a tree. A metaphor's usual form is A is B, meaning A is like B: *I am a worm. He is an ass. God is our rock.*

It also has other forms, such as B of A. *Cup of salvation* (meaning that salvation is a cup) and *bread of wickedness* are examples. Another form is *this dead dog* (instead of saying, *This man is a dead dog*). Or the metaphor may be an action: *He has girded me with gladness* (instead of, *gladness is my girdle*).

All these metaphors suggest that there is one point of comparison between two things that in the main are unlike. Consider the last one above. How is gladness like a girdle, or belt? What does a belt do? It holds up clothes and makes a man ready to work or do business. There is a sort of strength and security in it. Likewise gladness gives strength and security to the spirit.

Look at these references and think about each one: Joshua 1:8; 2 Kings 7:2; Job 13:25; 41:14; Psalm 109:29; Isaiah 1:31; 7:4; Matthew 26:26; Luke 11:39; 2 Corinthians 5:1-4; Ephesians 1:18.

2. *Simile.* A simile is much like a metaphor, except that the comparison is actually expressed, using the words *like* or *as.* If we would say, "I am like a worm" or "God is like a rock to us," the meaning would be the same as in the metaphors above. The metaphor is more vivid, yet perhaps not quite so clear and more easily misunderstood.

Job 41:24 is a simile: "His heart is hard as a stone." This statement even shows the point of comparison: Each item is hard. Of course we know that one is physical hardness, the other non-physical. It is a vivid, emphatic way of giving the truth of heart-hardness, that is to say, of stubbornness or strength of will.

Most similes give the point of comparison as this one does, but some say only that two things are alike and leave us to discover in what way. For example, Micah 7:4 states that "the best of them is like a brier." In what way like a brier? Since the text does not say plainly, we have to study the context to see what the point of comparison is.

Often things in nature are used for comparison. One quality of an object may be used for one simile while another is used for a different simile. Sometimes a good quality and a bad quality give opposite similes. Hosea 6:4, "your love . . . is like the dew that goes early away," refers to dew's ephemeral quality. The verse describes unfaithful love. In Hosea 14:5, God says, "I will be as the dew to Israel." And the next lines show he has in mind dew's good quality of giving life and growth to plants. So we cannot assume that the quality mentioned in one passage will necessarily be the same as in another. We must interpret each simile in its context. (See various similes using *dove:* Ps. 55:6; Is. 59:11; Jer. 48:28; Hos. 7:11.)

Here are some references to study which include similes of actions, not just of quality: Judges 7:12; Psalm 59:6; 92:12; 133:2-3; Proverbs 10:26; Isaiah 9:18-19; Jeremiah 17:6; Matthew 17:20; 25:32-33; Luke 17:24; 1 Peter 2:2.

Guidelines for Interpretation

We can use these steps in interpreting the figures of comparison:

1. *Notice whether the point of comparison is mentioned in the verse or context.* If it is, take that as the key to interpretation; for example, in 1 Kings 12:4, the people say to Rehoboam, "Your father made our yoke heavy." We can see from the context what they meant.

2. *If the point of comparison is not mentioned, consider the objects being compared and take the natural meaning as the most likely one.* Isaiah 1:30, "You shall be ... like a garden without water." What would such a garden be, especially in the summer? It would be dead, of course. That is the natural meaning of the image, and the context confirms the meaning of destruction.

3. *Use parallel passages (if there are any).* Remembering that an object may have different meanings in different similes, use care. Do not use imagination so freely you arrive at strange interpretations. In Matthew 11:29 Jesus says, "Take my yoke upon you." It is obviously a metaphor. But what does it mean? We need not speculate to get some hidden meaning. Don't Genesis 27:40; Isaiah 47:6; and Jeremiah 27:8; 28:14 indicate plainly the meaning of having someone's yoke upon you?

Figures of Relation

Next we will consider two figures of speech where one word is substituted for another which is related to it. A is mentioned but B is meant.

3. *Metonymy.* Metonymy is a figure of speech in which an idea is evoked or named by means of a term designating some associated notion. The two words may be related as *cause and effect* ("mine arrow is incurable," Job 34:6 AV, where arrow is used for the wound caused by the arrow); as *a sign for something signified* ("the key of David," Rev. 3:7, where key is substituted for the authority it represents); as *an author for his writing* ("whenever Moses is read," 2 Cor. 3:15, where Moses is mentioned to represent his writing); or as *a place used for people* ("there went out . . . all the country of Judea," Mt. 3:5, where Judea stands for its people).

Other references to investigate are Genesis 49:10; Deuteronomy 17:6 (AV); Joshua 10:21; Proverbs 10:21; Jeremiah 21:7, 10; Hosea 1:2; Acts 6:7; 11:23; 1 Corinthians 10:21.

4. *Synecdoche.* Synecdoche is a figure of speech by which a more inclusive term is used for a less inclusive term or vice versa. A part is put for the whole, or the whole for a part; singular for plural, or plural for singular. Genesis 42:38 (AV), "Then shall ye bring down my grey hairs with sorrow to the grave." The speaker has in mind not only his hairs but all of himself. "Bring me down to the grave" is the meaning. A part is given for the whole. Jeremiah 25:29, "I am summoning a sword against all the inhabitants of the earth." One sword only? No, one represents many; the singular is used for the plural.

For further study consider Joshua 7:1, 11; 1 Samuel 14:45; 2 Samuel 16:21; Job 29:11; Isaiah 2:4; Matthew 6:11; 12:40 (is this whole for part?).

To interpret uses of metonymy and synecdoche use these two guidelines:

1. *Observe carefully.* Does the literal meaning make non-

sense or confusion? Isaiah 22:22 says, "I will place on his shoulder the key of the house of David." We laugh when we picture this literally, but as a figure it shows authority and importance.

2. *Use the context and the situation in the passage to arrive at the figurative meaning.* Deuteronomy 19:15 (AV) speaks of "the mouth of two witnesses." Studying the context, what does *mouth* mean? It stands for "speaking, giving testimony."

Other Figures of Speech

5. *Apostrophe.* In this figure of speech a writer addresses directly things or persons absent or imaginary. And for the purpose of the moment he treats things as if they were persons. "Why look you with envy, O many peaked mountain?" (Ps. 68:16). Notice how the psalmist talks to the mountain as though it can hear and think. "Sing, O barren one" (Is. 54:1) is another example; the context shows that the Lord is speaking to a nation, not to a woman. Apostrophe is a dramatic figure that adds life and strength to writing. It is normally quite obvious; and since the context usually shows it is not literal, it offers no real problem of interpretation.

Other references are 2 Samuel 18:33; 1 Kings 13:2; Isaiah 14:12; Jeremiah 22:29; 47:6; Ezekiel 37:4. The Old Testament prophets used this figure a great deal.

6. *Personification.* In this figure of speech a writer speaks *about* (but not *to*) a non-personal or non-living thing as though it were a person; that is, he attributes personal characteristics to things which do not have them. Psalm 98:8, "Let the floods clap their hands." The writer knows that floods do not have hands. He knows, and we know, that he is giving a lovely figure, a dramatic way of saying that nature too is blessed by the presence of God.

Personification is often combined with apostrophe. We read in Deuteronomy 32:1, "Give ear, O heavens" and in Isaiah 44:23, "Sing, O heavens." Since the literal meaning is impossible, and often ridiculous, we can usually recognize the figure without difficulty. But how do we interpret it? Consider Psalm 19:2: "Day to day pours forth speech." Days do not talk, but in verse 1 the verbs *are telling* and *proclaims* are parallel, and the whole passage is saying that nature reveals God and his work. So the context makes the meaning clear.

Other references are Joshua 24:27; Psalm 77:16; 114:3; Proverbs 1:20; 6:22; Jeremiah 14:7; 46:10; Matthew 6:34; James 1:15.

7. *Hyperbole.* Hyperbole is deliberate exaggeration for emphasis. Both writer and reader must recognize it as deliberate. Otherwise the reader might suspect the author of deceit or of handling truth carelessly. When the psalmist said, "My eyes shed streams of tears" (Ps. 119:136), he was not speaking literally. Rivers were not flowing from his eyes. He was deeply grieved because men were not keeping God's law; and this figure expressed his intense hurt.

Again, can we suppose that God meant it to be taken literally when he said that "the sound of a driven leaf shall put . . . to flight" the exiles from Israel (Lev. 26:36)? Rather, this shows the pitiful condition they will experience in exile: They will live in fear and danger. The context normally shows the meaning of hyperbole if it is not plain in the sentence itself.

Read also Deuteronomy 1:28; 1 Kings 1:40; 2 Samuel 1:23; Psalm 119:20; Jeremiah 19:4; 23:9; John 21:25.

8. *Interrogation.* This figure of speech is a special kind of question—a query which can have only one answer. Because that answer is obvious, the writer need not give it. In Jeremiah 32:27, God asks, "I am the Lord, the God of all flesh; is anything too hard for me?" This is not a question for debate. The reader cannot say, "Maybe yes and maybe no." The only answer is No. The question really says the same thing Jeremiah himself says in verse 17 of the same chapter, "Nothing is too hard for thee." God, too, could

have made a statement in verse 27, but by asking a question the point comes more strongly to the reader. He himself has to make the point by answering in his own mind; he does not simply hear God make it. This figure is used a great deal in reasoning discourse and is often simply called a rhetorical question.

Interrogation can be used for different purposes. Sometimes it calls attention to something, sometimes it introduces a topic. Psalm 8:4, "What is man that thou art mindful of him?" Jeremiah 23:29, "Is not my word like fire?" Interrogation usually creates no problem of interpretation. The meaning can be seen by turning the question around into a statement. For example, my word is like a fire.

Verses for study are Job 21:22; Jeremiah 2:11; 13:23; 30:6; Amos 3:3-4; Obadiah 1:5; Matthew 7:16; 1 Corinthians 10:22.

9. *Irony.* This figure is different from the others, for it says the opposite of what it means. It is used for emphasis. Like hyperbole, it must be clear to the hearers so there is no question of deceit. If irony is spoken, the speaker's tone of voice reveals it. Since we have written rather than spoken words in the Bible, we may have some difficulty recognizing irony.

In 2 Samuel 6:20 King David's wife says, "How the king of Israel honored himself today." The rest of the verse shows quite clearly that she really meant he had dishonored himself. In 1 Kings 22:15 the Lord's prophet foretells success for the proposed expedition, just as the false prophets had done. He obviously speaks in irony, however, for the context shows that he knows the armies will be unsuccessful. If verse 15 is not irony, then the prophet is lying.

It is difficult to tell whether some passages are ironic, but most are plain. When you are uncertain, think carefully about both possibilities. Consider it as a straightforward statement and see whether that meaning makes good sense in the context. Then think of it as irony. Usually the choice will be clear.

Other references are Numbers 24:11; 1 Kings 18:27; Job 12:2; 38:21; Zechariah 11:13 (lordly!); 1 Corinthians 4:8; 2 Corinthians 11:19.

Three other figures of speech occur infrequently and so are not as important as the others. *Euphemism* is substituting a more agreeable expression for something unpleasant or taboo. Acts 7:60 uses the phrase *he fell asleep* instead of *he died.* Judges 19:22 uses *that we may know him* for homosexuality. *Litotes* is stating something by denying its opposite, as we might say *not far off* when we mean *near.* In Psalm 51:17 *thou wilt not despise* means *thou wilt accept.* In 1 Samuel 26:8 *I will not strike him twice* means *I will kill him with the first blow.* *Pleonasm* is the use of superfluous words, as in 2 Samuel 7:22, "we have heard with our ears," or Deuteronomy 3:27, "Behold it with your eyes." In some translations the unnecessary words are dropped.

Figures of speech add beauty, vividness and emphasis to language. If we can recognize and interpret them in the Bible, God's Word will come to us with greater strength and clarity. In fact recognizing them may help us to understand verses that otherwise may appear to be contradictory. God's Word is rich with meaning. Thank him for these figures that add to our comprehension of that meaning.

14 Symbols

We can define a symbol as anything which suggests or stands for a meaning in addition to its ordinary one. It may be something natural like a dove, or something manufactured, like a cross. We use symbols in our ordinary life. People wear signs or badges to represent achievements. The way a man wears his hair may symbolize an attitude he wants to show. Spies and government agents use words whose special meaning is known only to their fellows.

The Bible uses symbols, too. They may be natural or miraculous. They may be things that actually exist or things seen in a vision. They may be objects (like salt or lampstands), actions (like eating a roll or building a miniature city), ordinances (like baptism or the Passover), materials (like white linen), numbers, colors, names (like Sodom or Egypt—used for Jerusalem), metals (like gold or brass), jewels (like a pearl), creatures (like a lion or a dove) or other things.

Symbols can be used either to reveal truth or to hide it. They hide truth from those who do not understand the symbolic meaning and see only the natural one. The Bible often does not identify its symbols but leaves it to the reader to recognize them. So we have to study carefully, neither overlooking symbols nor seeing symbols that are not there.

Symbols can be the means of expressing truth, but we can make serious errors if we do not recognize them.

The metaphors of the Scripture are often symbols—for example, "this is my body . . . this is my blood" (Mk. 14:22, 24). We easily recognize the metaphor here and the fact that the bread is a symbol of Christ's body and the wine of his blood. A basic meaning is clear in the context: Because his body was broken and his blood poured out in his death, we break the bread and pour out the wine to symbolize that death. But there is another meaning, too. Why do we eat and drink? Many passages, such as John 6:32-35, 48-63; 7:37-39, show that our eating and drinking are symbolic acts. Symbols of what? If we take literally Jesus' words to eat his flesh and drink his blood (Jn. 6:53), then he is demanding cannibalism, one of the most degrading acts of fallen, sinful man. Recognizing symbols can save us from sad mistakes.

The same object may symbolize more than one thing, as water speaks both of cleansing and of destruction. We should not assume that the meaning of a symbol in one passage will be the same in all. *Red* is commonly thought to be a symbol of Christ's blood and therefore of his atonement. It is rather surprising, however, to examine the verses where this word and its synonyms *crimson* and *scarlet* occur. In Isaiah 63:2 it is used for judgment; in Isaiah 1:18, for sin; in Proverbs 23:31, wine is red; in Matthew 16:2, the sky; and in Nahum 2:3, the soldiers. It seems that no passage clearly declares that this color symbolizes the death of Christ. If we believe that meaning we must do it without plain scriptural evidence and therefore hold it as possible rather than certain. What about *serpent* (Jn. 3:14; Rev. 20:2)?

Symbolic Numbers

The Bible uses some numbers symbolically. The most prominent number is seven. No verse says it is symbolic, but when we study the verses in which it is used we sense an implication beyond the literal meaning. To consider all the verses is difficult—since there are over 600—but you can look up the following: Genesis 29:18; 41:2, 18; 50:10; Exodus 12:15; 25:37; Leviticus 4:6; 26:24; Numbers 23:1; Deuteronomy 28:7; Joshua 6:4; Ruth 4:15; Psalm 119:164; Proverbs 24:16; 26:16; Zechariah 4:2; Matthew 12:45; Acts 6:3; and Revelation 1:4. These verses show that the number seven often carries a force of completion, perfection, totality. There are many verses in which this extra meaning is not present, however, so we must consider every occurrence individually.

Other numbers that are used symbolically are *three* (often related to the Trinity—Num. 6:24-27; Is. 6:3; Mt. 28:19; 2 Cor. 13:14; Rev. 4:8); *four* (often related to the fullness of the earth or physical creation—Jer. 49:36; Ezek. 37:9; Is. 11:12; Lk. 13:29; Rev. 7:1); *twelve* (often related to groups of God's people—Gen. 49:28; Ex. 28:21; Josh. 4:9; Mt. 10:1; Rev. 21:12, 14); and *forty* (often related to testing or judgment—Gen. 7:4; Ex. 24:18; Num. 14:34; Deut. 8:1-5; Mt. 4:2).

These numbers, and probably some others, are used symbolically in the Scripture, but we should not think that every occurrence of each of them is symbolic. Otherwise the seven sons of Job represent perfection and the three daughters divinity. In Isaiah 6:3 *holy, holy, holy* may symbolize the Trinity, but there seems to be no clear significance in the three months that Moses was hid by his parents (Acts 7:20) or the three days that Paul was without sight (Acts 9:9). We must not see extra meaning in a verse unless there is some indication that it is there.

Guidelines for Interpretation
Since there are many instances of symbols in the Bible, some guidelines for approaching them will help.

1. *Study the way the Bible itself interprets symbols.* Notice *lion* in 1 Peter 5:8 and *rain* in Isaiah 55:10-11. Already we have

seen the word *dew* in Hosea 6:4 and 14:5, and each of those similes has a different symbolic meaning. If it is a general symbol, such as a color, use a concordance to look up as many references as you can and see to what extent the Scripture suggests one or more symbolic meanings. You may want to keep in your notes (or even in a separate notebook) a list of symbols that you find as you study.

2. *When studying natural objects, note their natural qualities.* In these the symbolic meaning will be found; for example, *lamb* suggests meekness, *salt* speaks of preservation, a *pig* means filth. See which quality gives the meaning in the passage you are studying.

3. *Study the context.* The context is the main help in determining the meaning of symbols. For instance, Jeremiah 24:1-3 describes Jeremiah's vision of two baskets of figs, one with good figs, the other with bad. In verses 4-10, the Lord explains the symbol: The figs represent two groups of people. The exiles are the good figs; the king and the others who remained in the city are the bad.

4. *Avoid speculation or arbitrary meanings that come from your own head and not from the Scripture.* If there is no direct evidence for a meaning you think of, the most you can say is that it is a *possible* meaning. You cannot dogmatically say it is *the* meaning.

Some interesting passages that *perhaps* have symbols in them are Exodus 13:21; Psalm 69:2 with Isaiah 44:3; Ezekiel 1:13 with Hebrews 12:29; Ezekiel 37:1-4; Micah 4:13 with Psalm 107:16; Matthew 17:2 with Revelation 19:8.

15   Types

Types are an important and rather complicated area of biblical interpretation. Bible students do not always agree on the questions relating to types. Yet types beautifully bring out aspects of the Scripture's truth that are valuable for us to know.

Types are of various kinds: *persons* (like Adam, Moses, Elijah, Melchizedek), *events* (like the lifting up of the brazen serpent and the flood), *objects* (like the altar of sacrifice, the lamb, the incense), *institutions* (like the Passover and other feasts), *places* (like Canaan and Jerusalem) and *offices* (like prophet and priest).

A type can be defined as a divinely purposed, Old Testament foreshadowing of a New Testament spiritual reality. Three key points are here.

1. *The type is divinely purposed.* We must see evidence in Scripture that God has indicated the correspondence between the type and its fulfillment. Where the New Testament speaks of the parallel there can be no doubt. If the New Testament makes no mention of it, then we must be careful. In such a case, the correspondence must be so clear that there is no reasonable doubt. There may be minor parallels in many things of the Old and New Testaments, and people who have good imaginations can find more than

others can. Biblical interpretation, however, cannot depend on imagination. We must consider the evidence and take as types those parallels that are so clear that they cannot be just chance.

2. *The type is in the Old Testament; the fulfillment (called the anti-type) is in the New.* This makes the type distinct from other figures like symbols and parables, where the spiritual meaning can apply to the same time as the event.

3. *The type is a "shadow."* It may be physically real, as the tabernacle was; nevertheless, it is still only a shadow when compared with the spiritual reality that fulfills it. In a photo of a tree, there is no "tree reality" in the picture, though there is "paper reality" and "chemical reality"; yet the photo is a likeness of a real tree. Similarly, the tabernacle actually existed—it had its own physical reality and meaning—but it also had a meaning that pointed forward to the ultimate reality of Christ as the way to God.

Quite often a type includes one or more symbols, so we consider their interpretation within the type. For example, the high priest is a type of Christ. What may his linen garment symbolize (Ex. 28:39; Heb. 4:14)? The New Testament may not apply the symbol in speaking of the type.

The first, perhaps the main, problem is how to recognize the types that are not identified by the New Testament. Among Bible students there are two extreme views on the matter. Some believe that we should consider as types only those the New Testament refers to as types. This view is based on the conviction that God must name the types, that when we call other things types we are just using our imagination, not interpreting the Bible. Others believe that practically everything in the Old Testament points to the New; therefore a typical meaning can be found in most details. At least the meaning is there, though we may not discover it.

It is a sound principle of interpretation that we should find the meaning that is in the Scripture, not read meaning into it. Therefore, it seems wise to take a moderate position on the question of types, accepting those the New Testament identifies and any others where the parallel of Old Testament fact and New Testament reality is so clear that it could not have occurred by chance. Of course, each Bible student has to use his prayerful judgment about the clearness of such parallels, so he may not be dogmatic or critical of those who differ with him.

Jesus explained to the two disciples (Lk. 24:47) things concerning himself from *all* the Old Testament Scriptures. During that Sunday afternoon walk, he could not possibly have discussed every passage (every incident, every person) in the Old Testament. This verse cannot be pressed to mean that everything in the Old Testament is directly typical, but it does show that the Old Testament is full of Christ.

New Testament Interpretation

To help us in looking at the parallels we can first observe how the New Testament interprets some types.

1. *Lifting up the brazen serpent in the wilderness* (Jn. 3:14-15). We will first list the facts that are recorded in Numbers 21, then note those that are said to be parallel with the New Testament truth.

Numbers 21:4-9	*John 3:14-15*
The people complained	No mention
God sent fiery serpents, many people died	No mention
People confessed, we have sinned	No mention
Moses prayed for them	No mention
God commanded him to make a fiery serpent	Christ was lifted up
Moses made a serpent of brass and put it on a pole	No mention of the brass symbol
Anyone who looked was healed	Whoever believes will have eternal life

Notice that the New Testament ignores most of the details of the Old Testament incident. This does not mean that they cannot have typical meaning, but it shows that the interpretation given in Scripture is not concerned with them. It is concerned with this main fact: The serpent was lifted up, people looked at it and were healed. Some Bible students feel that the words *as Moses lifted up the serpent* give authority for finding meaning in the other details. Perhaps so, but we should keep in mind that the Scripture itself does not tell us this meaning.

2. *The Passover.* Again let us tabulate the features of the type and the New Testament interpretation.

Exodus 12:3-13	*1 Corinthians 5:7-8*
One lamb sacrificed per house	Christ sacrificed
A one-year-old male taken from the sheep or goats on the tenth day and held till the fourteenth	No mention
Lamb killed in the *evening*	No mention
Blood sprinkled on the doorposts and lintel	No mention
Flesh eaten roasted	No mention
Flesh eaten with unleavened bread and bitter herbs	Christians are to eat with unleavened bread of sincerity and truth
Leftovers burned; all consumed	No mention
Meal eaten in haste—loins girded, sandals on feet, staff in hand	No mention
God saw the blood and passed over	No mention

Note the interpretation that the Bible itself makes. Some other obvious parallels are not pointed out: The sacrifice is a male, killed in the evening; God passes over where he sees the sacrifice's blood applied. Some find parallels in other things as well, but the Scripture nowhere mentions them.

Possible Unidentified Types
It is important to consider some incidents that many students consider to be types, but which the New Testament does not mention. One of the most important is Abraham's offering of Isaac on Mt. Moriah, as recorded in Genesis 22.

The facts are familiar. God told Abraham to go to the mountain and sacrifice his son. Abraham obeyed: On the mountain he prepared an altar and put Isaac on it to kill him. Then God stopped him, telling him that by his action he had shown his obedience. God provided a substitute for Isaac, a ram, which Abraham sacrificed before returning home with Isaac. The thrust of the story is Abraham's test and his obedience.

The New Testament comments on this twice. In Hebrews 11:17-19 we read that Abraham was tried and by faith offered Isaac. He believed that God could raise this child of promise from the dead, and figuratively speaking he received Isaac back by resurrection. James 2:21-22 says that Abraham was justified by works in offering Isaac and that by his works his faith was perfected. In neither of these passages is there any suggestion that the incident pictures God's offering of his Son Christ on the cross. The message concerns Abraham's experience with God: being tested, showing faith and giving obedience. And though there was a substitute offered in sacrifice on the altar, it was a substitute for the son; the son was not a substitute for another. This is the reverse of the anti-type, where Christ is a substitute for sinners.

So if we say this is a type of Christ's death, we must say that the typical meaning is possible, not certain. And we must lay the emphasis where the Scripture puts it. Both Genesis and the New Testament passages emphasize the test and obedience of Abraham. To make Isaac's sacrifice a type of Christ's death is to change this emphasis. We may speak of Abraham's sacrifice in giving his son, but his being tested and obedient does not fit the anti-type, for God the Father cannot be tested by nor be obedient to anyone greater than himself.

Another well-known story is that of Joseph. From his boyhood until he became ruler of Egypt, there is a surprising number of details that parallel details in the life of

Christ. We can study Genesis 37—50, list these details and then consider whether so many parallels could be accidental. If not, then we can legitimately consider Joseph as a type of Christ.

In Galatians 4:21-31 an Old Testament story is given a spiritual or typical meaning. Some students consider this an allegory rather than a type, but a few points are taken from the story of Hagar and Ishmael, Sarah and Isaac, and a parallel is drawn. So we conclude that types need not have one point; however, that is the way the New Testament usually interprets them.

Guidelines for Interpretation

It will help to notice some guidelines for studying types:

1. *With the exception of a few visions, the types are actual things in history, and the anti-types, too, usually have a historical basis.* The Passover in Israel's history pointed forward to the historical (but spiritually significant) death of Christ.

2. *Types are physical pictures prefiguring spiritual realities.* In the example in John 3:14 physically seeing the serpent is typical of spiritually seeing Christ through faith.

3. *The fulfillment is on a higher level than the type.* See John 1:29. How much greater is the Lamb of God than an animal!

4. *There is a central point in the comparison, though in a few cases some secondary details, too.* This we saw in discussing John 3:14-15 and 1 Corinthians 5:7-8.

5. *The spiritual fulfillment grows out of the natural meaning of the type.* There should be a natural parallel, not an arbitrary or fanciful connection. As Moses—so the Son of Man. A couple of quotations will show what interpreters can find when they disregard this principle.

One writes this about the Passover lamb: "Now, the lamb taken on the tenth day, and kept up until the fourteenth day, shows us Christ foreordained of God from eternity, but manifest for us in time." Is there any evidence for this?

Another takes some of the clean animals as typical (Lev. 11:4-6): "The act of chewing the cud is probably a method of describing a good conversation such as should characterize true Christians. A true Christian will talk right (chewing the cud), and will walk right (dividing the hoof)." And again, "Chewing the cud refers to meditating on the Scriptures and talking about the things of God and the things that are pleasing in God's sight. It refers to godly meditations as in Psalm 1:2, etc. If we walk with the Lord and talk about the things of God, then we are 'clean' Christians, and acceptable in God's sight." In verse 7 of the chapter it is mentioned that the pig divides the hoof but does not chew the cud. Does the pig, therefore, have a "clean" walk, even though his talk is not right? We must beware of arbitrary conclusions.

6. *Do not base types on such things as colors, numbers, materials, shape, etc.* If there is a clear type and a detail like a number fits in with it, well and good—but let the type rest on something more basic than a number.

7. *Avoid dogmatism when the New Testament does not speak clearly.*

Here are some passages that may or may not be typical. Study them prayerfully.

Genesis 2:2-3: God's rest a type of the Christian's spiritual rest in Christ?

Genesis 7:1-5: The ark a type of salvation in Christ?

Exodus 30:17-21: The laver a type of washing from sin?

Leviticus 4: The sin-offering a type of Christ's atonement?

Deuteronomy 18:15: Moses a type of Christ as prophet?

1 Kings 17:12: Two sticks a type of the cross?

Hebrews 9:24: The tabernacle a type of Christ, the way to God?

Types and Symbols

Before we leave this topic, it will help to add a postscript summarizing the differences between symbols and types, since they overlap.

1. A type is actual (historical) while a symbol may not be.

2. A type is in the Old Testament with its fulfillment in the New. A symbol has no time reference.

3. A type is particular (one thing or event). A symbol may be general.

4. A type may have some details, though not usually. A symbol has one point.

5. A type may contain one or more symbols.

16 Parables and Allegories

A parable is usually described as a story told with the purpose of giving some moral or spiritual truth. It is true to life but not usually an actual occurrence. Someone has called a parable "an earthly story with a heavenly meaning." We can also call it an extended simile, for it is a comparison. Often in the Gospels Jesus begins parables with the words *The kingdom of heaven may be compared to.* (See, for instance, Mt. 22:1.) Many parables, however, do not have that beginning, as in Matthew 21:33; "Hear another parable. There was a householder...."

There are some parables in the Old Testament, but mainly they are found in the first three Gospels. The Gospel of John has none, though John does give some allegories, as in chapters 10 and 15.

Parables have three elements: the setting, story and application. In some of Christ's parables the setting is missing, or at least is not directly given, and in others the application. In some there is only the story. Christ told the parable of the Good Samaritan in response to a question from a lawyer, and at the end he applied the message (Lk. 10:25-37). In Matthew 21:33-41 the controversy over authority is the setting and the threat of judgment the application. In Matthew 13:3-9 and Luke 13:18-19 one or two elements are missing—in the first case the setting, and in the second both the setting and application. Where both setting and application are part of the context of the story, the interpretation of the parable is easier; without one or both of them we have more difficulty.

Often the setting gives the key to the interpretation. For instance, in Luke 15 it is the objections of the Pharisees and scribes that impel Jesus to tell the three parables. All three parables focus on the lesson that God rejoices when sinners come to repentance, so there should be no objection when Jesus receives them.

Parables normally have one main point. We do not try to find a spiritual lesson in the various details but look for the central message. We do this because of the way Jesus himself applies his parables. In Luke 15, Jesus applies the parable of the Lost Sheep: "There will be more joy in heaven over one sinner who repents than over ninety-nine righteous persons who need no repentance" (v. 7). Verse 10 gives the same interpretation of the next parable. Essentially it is the same for the Prodigal Son, even though there are more details in that story. How does Jesus interpret the parable of the Good Samaritan? He gets the lawyer to make the interpretation: It was the Samaritan who proved to be a neighbor. "Go and do likewise," said Jesus. He suggests no special meaning for the thieves, the other two men, the donkey, the money or the innkeeper.

Jesus does not always make only one point from a parable. Jesus applies several details in the parables of the Sower and of the Tares and the Wheat (Mt. 13). The same is true of the story of the Laborers in the Vineyard (Mt. 20). While we might profitably study why these are different, we must see that they are exceptions to the general rule that a parable has one main lesson.

In the early years of the Christian era, some theologians who allegorized passages of Scripture found wonderful meaning in the details of the parables. Origen, who was one of these theologians, offered this interpretation of the Good Samaritan: Adam is the man who fell among thieves. Jerusalem stands for heaven, Jericho for the world. The robbers are the devil and his angels, while the priest stands for the law and the Levite for the prophets. Christ, of course, is the Good Samaritan, his body the beast, his church the inn. Father and Son are the two denarii. Christ's second coming is the Samaritan's promise to come again. This interpretation fits at least some features, but there is not even a hint in the passage to suggest this interpretation —and in fact, Jesus gives a different one. So Origen's interpretation has no basis in Scripture, and this should make us wary about following him.

Jesus probably told some parables several times. The Lost Sheep is found in two different settings. In Matthew 18 it is related to God's care for children, while in Luke 15 to his concern for sinners. In both cases, however, God's loving care is highlighted.

Guidelines for Interpretation

1. *Think first of the story's natural meaning.* The spiritual lesson must be based on that.

2. *Note the occasion of the parable if the occasion is given.* For example, examine the situation that gave rise to Jesus' short parable in the Pharisee's house (Lk. 7:41-43). You need not be bothered if the setting is not clear, for you can get the meaning from other things. If the setting is clear, it is important; and you must see the message of the parable in relation to it.

3. *Find the main teaching, the central point.* This is derived either from the application Jesus makes or from the story itself. Jesus told the story of the Ten Virgins, then gave the interpretation: Watch for my coming, for you do not know the day or the hour. We can also infer from the story that those who are ready will leave with him.

4. *Check the meaning with the direct teaching of Scripture.*

Since parables are figurative language, we do not use them to establish teaching or doctrine; but they confirm and strengthen the truth that is given elsewhere in Scripture. For instance, if we used the Prodigal Son to establish how a sinner gets back to God, then repentance would be sufficient and there would be no need for Christ's atonement.

5. *If there are any problems in understanding the story, get what light you can from the cultural and historical background.* For example, many students know that it was the custom for a host to give wedding garments to his guests. This explains why the man without one was judged so severely (Mt. 22:11-13): He must not have taken what was provided.

The Vineyard Laborers

Let us apply these guidelines to one of the parables, the Laborers in the Vineyard (Mt. 20:1-16).

First follow the basic principle of reading and observing the passage along with sufficient context. Since verse 1 starts with *for*, we realize that the parable connects with chapter 19 and that the chapter division is not helpful. Notice the last verse of chapter 19 and connect it with verse 16 of chapter 20. What are the significant words in these verses? Do you find those same words in the parable story (see vv. 8, 10, 12, 14)? Can you see the links that are indicated by the *for* in 20:1 and the *so* in 20:16?

Next consider how the story may shed light on these two verses. Does anything last in the story become first, or the first last? Did the last laborers come in first? Of course, they were paid first, but did they get ahead in another way? What about the comparative hourly wage?

Why should the householder give the last laborers such good treatment? Compare the terms of service for the two groups (vv. 2 and 7). Do you see a different spirit in the two groups? Go back to chapter 19 and see what spirit Peter showed, remembering that what he said gave occasion for Jesus to tell the parable. Did the rich young ruler (19:22) show a spirit like Peter's? Perhaps the words *have* and *receive* in 19:21, 27, 29 and 20:9-10 may suggest a link. Can you now state the central teaching of the parable?

We have noticed carefully the parable's setting and the application given by Jesus. We have sought to observe carefully repeated words and linking words. The parable in its context gives a strong message—a solemn warning to any like Peter who are concerned too much with what they will receive. Beware, says Jesus, because those who are first may come in last in the end.

Here are some other Gospel parables to study:

Mark 4:30-32: The Mustard Seed

Luke 7:41-43: The Two Debtors

Luke 11:5-8: The Friend at Midnight

Luke 16:19-31: The Rich Man and Lazarus (Is this a parable?)

Luke 18:1-8: The Unjust Judge

Allegories

It is good to look at allegories along with parables because they are somewhat similar. An allegory has been called an extended metaphor. The simple metaphor says A is B. With A, C and E designating related parts of a story or picture, an allegory says A is B, C is D and E is F. In John 10 the allegory is more a story; in chapter 15 it is more a picture.

In John 15 Jesus says, "I am the true vine, and my Father is the vinedresser, . . . you are the branches" (vv. 1, 5). This is the basic structure of the allegory. Then Jesus gives a spiritual meaning to other features of this relationship: Branches are to abide in the vine and bear fruit; the vinedresser prunes the branches that bear fruit and takes away the ones that do not; the fruit brings glory to the vinedresser.

We can find the basic interpretation within this allegory. We need not go outside it. (For that reason, an allegory often is simpler to interpret than some other language forms.) This does not mean that everything in the allegory is plain. Some features are left without interpretation, and we have the problem of finding the right meaning. Branches that are barren are taken out and burned. What is the spiritual parallel of that? Verse 6 states this as a terrible reality but does not show its clear meaning for us. So we have to seek it.

John 10 contains the allegory of the Good Shepherd and the Sheep. Let us list the features and the interpretations given:

Shepherd	Jesus
Sheep	No mention
Gatekeeper	No mention
Fold	No mention
Door	Jesus
Robbers	Those who "came before" Jesus
Stranger	No mention
Wolf	No mention
Hireling	No mention

It is striking that Jesus gives little of the meaning in this allegory, leaving it to us to find it. He does scarcely more than identify himself as both shepherd and door. We still have to learn who those are who came before him. There are suggestions in the passage for interpreting other features. He knows his sheep and they know his voice, which indicates they are believers (his disciples). Robbers who do not go through the door must be false religious leaders, who do not acknowledge Jesus. The hireling, too, is a false shepherd, therefore, a religious leader. But fold, wolf and stranger are left unidentified. We may conclude from this that it is not necessary to find meaning in every detail. Though in an allegory some details do have meaning, there is still, as in a parable, a focus on certain main points, as we see in Jesus' interpretation in John 10.

Some Old Testament allegories are Psalm 80:8-15; Proverbs 5:15-20; Ecclesiastes 12:3-7.

Guidelines for Interpretation

1. *Note the details, or features, of the allegory.* It is good to list them, as we did with John 10.

2. *Note the interpretation given for any of the features.* List these also.

3. *Consider other features, seeing if a likely meaning can be derived for them from other passages.* For example, are the individual metaphors used elsewhere in the Bible? Be slow to make a dogmatic interpretation on this basis, however, remembering that the same object can be used in metaphors with opposite meaning. Consider such interpretation of the features of an allegory as possible, not certain.

4. *Do not try to identify all the features.* Christ did not do so for the allegories in John 10 and 15. Consider only interpretations that are quite clear, not doubtful. Do not make forced or fanciful ones.

17 Hebrew Idioms

An *idiom* is an expression peculiar to one particular language. Each language has different ways of saying things. Idioms reveal thought patterns of the people who speak the language.

In Hindi people say, "Ikkis bis ka farq (or antar) hai," which literally means "It is the difference between 20 and 21." This actually means "scarcely any difference at all"; hence it is roughly equivalent to the English idiom "six of one and half a dozen of the other." In the Uduk language of the Sudan people do not say "Let not your heart be troubled," but rather, "Don't keep a shiver in your liver." For they think of the liver as the seat of the emotions.

The Hebrew language has its idioms, too. Some of them are figures of speech, but because they are distinct in Hebrew thinking, we will consider them in this chapter. They are found in the New Testament as well as the Old, for the writers of the New Testament were mainly Hebrews.

There are more in the AV than in modern versions, because the recent translations often have sought to make clear by putting it into our own idiom. In Ezekiel 44:12 (AV), for example, God says concerning the unfaithful Levites, "I have lifted up mine hand against them." Since the hand was raised to take a solemn oath (as in court), the RSV translates, "I have sworn concerning them." This is not wrong, provided that the new idiom accurately expresses the original thought. Great care must be taken to safeguard that.

Suppose a Uduk Christian were reading from his Bible and translating it into English for us. Suppose he translated John 14:1 as "Don't keep a shiver in your liver." We would not understand him. The literal translation would not give us the real thought. So there are times when idioms must be interpreted as they are translated.

Some of these idioms have technical names. To get more information about them, check your dictionary.

1. *Anthropomorphism.* This means literally *man's form.* It is speaking about God as though he has a body even though he does not. We have picked up many of these idioms through knowing the Bible, so we may pray "Lord, keep your hand on my loved one" without realizing that we are using anthropomorphism. An anthropomorphism is really a metaphor, but a special one, and one prominent in the Bible. It is also found in most other languages, but because of its distinctive use by the Hebrews we will consider it as a Hebrew idiom.

Many references, especially in the Old Testament, speak of God as having physical parts. *Face:* Exodus 33:23; Psalm 10:11; Jeremiah 21:10. *Eye: 2 Chronicles 7:16; Psalm 11:4;* Jeremiah 16:17. *Ear:* Psalm 10:17; Isaiah 37:17; Daniel 9:18. *Nose:* Exodus 15:8; Psalm 18:15; Isaiah 65:5. *Mouth:* 1 Kings 8:24; Isaiah 34:16; Micah 4:4. *Voice:* Job 40:9; Daniel 9:11, 14. *Arm:* Deuteronomy 11:2; Isaiah 62:8; Jeremiah 21:5. *Hand:* Exodus 33:23; Isaiah 50:2; Jeremiah 1:9. *Back:* Exodus 33:23; Isaiah 38:17; Jeremiah 18:17. *Soul and heart:* Genesis 6:6; 2 Chronicles 7:16; Psalm 11:5. *Feet:* Exodus 24:10; Psalm 77:19; Isaiah 60:13. *Form:* Psalm 17:15. Other forms of this idiom do not actually mention the body part, but imply it through action words like *sitting* and *walking.* (See Ps. 78:65; 113:5; Is. 26:21; Amos 7:7.)

We must remember that God in his own being does not have a body. In John 4:24 we read that God is a spirit and in Luke 24:39 that a spirit does not have flesh and bones. (Christ, the second Person of the Trinity, did take a body when he became incarnate; he is now a man as well as God.)

If all the above expressions are not literal, then what do they mean? The key is to ask what we use these members for. What do we do with our right arms? We work, which requires strength. And a man's right arm is usually stronger than his left. So to picture God's strength, the biblical writers, and even God himself, speak of his exercising power with his right arm. What do we do with our eyes! Through them we become aware of other people and of things. God's "eyes" suggest his awareness of us and of the creation. What do we do with our ears? We receive communication. That God's "ear is open" means he is ready to receive what we say.

In 2 Chronicles 16:9 we are startled to read that "the eyes of the LORD run to and fro throughout the whole earth." Literally, this is nonsense. Can you picture two (or more) gigantic eyes moving around the world like satellites or flying saucers? The truth expressed here is that God is aware of every faithful believer in any place in the world and is with that person to exercise power on his behalf. So using an anthropomorphism paints a picture of God's power and perfection.

With the passages relating to human form we can also link those that speak of God's having human feelings. God was sorry, remembered, repented (Gen. 6:6; 19:29; Jer. 18:8, 10, respectively). Such verses express a reality about God which is far beyond the actual human emotion. His repenting, however, is a special case. 1 Samuel 15:29 tells us that he is not a man that he should repent. Since God is unchangeable, in the strict sense he cannot repent. But God treats man on the basis of man's attitude, and if that attitude changes God's treatment changes. So it may seem that God repents as humans do, but in reality he does not. (See

Jer. 26:12-13.)

2. *Absolute for relative*. *Absolute* here means "free from relationship to other things"; *relative* means "having relation or comparison." *Matthew loves to eat steak* is an absolute statement. *Matthew prefers steak to chicken* is relative, for here the steak and chicken are being compared.

The Bible sometimes exchanges the absolute for the relative, commonly in the form: not A but B. An example is when Joseph tells his brothers, who sold him into Egypt, "It was not you who sent me here, but God" (Gen. 45:8). If this is literal, then it is not true. Joseph has already admitted (v. 5) that they sent him to Egypt and later he says that they meant it for evil (Gen. 50:20). So the statement is an idiom. Joseph means, "It wasn't *only* your doing, but God's also"; and God's sovereign purpose is what he wants to emphasize.

In some Bible passages it is very important to recognize this idiom. In Jeremiah 7:22-23 God says, "For in the day that I brought them out of the land of Egypt, I did not speak to your fathers or command them concerning burnt offerings and sacrifices. But this command I gave them, Obey my voice. . . ." Exodus and Leviticus say that God did speak about sacrifices when he brought the Hebrews out of Egypt. Liberals take this verse in Jeremiah to assert that Exodus and Leviticus are not historically accurate, but reflect some primitive, and mistaken, ideas about God. Jeremiah's statement, however, is a case of substituting the absolute for the relative. God did speak about sacrifices, but he was more concerned about the people's hearts and their obedience. If you want to see this idiom in other passages, look at Exodus 16:8; Deuteronomy 5:2-3; Psalm 51:16-17; 1 Corinthians 1:17; 9:9-10; Philippians 2:4; 1 John 3:18.

A different form of this idiom is in verses like Luke 14:26. Is one really to hate his family, even his wife, to follow Christ? That would contradict Ephesians 5:25 and many other passages. This is an absolute way of expressing a relative thought: All other loves and claims are to be put second, far behind one's devotion to Christ (compare Mt. 10:37). Consider also Romans 9:13.

How can you recognize this idiom? First, consider it as a literal statement. Does it make sense? If it does not, then consider it as an idiom. Study it in its context, and you will see some confirmation that you have the right meaning.

3. *Relative for absolute.* This is the opposite of the preceding idiom. Here the meaning is absolute but the form is comparative. In Luke 11:31-32 Jesus says that "something greater than Solomon [and] something greater than Jonah is here." Who or what is compared with Solomon and Jonah? It can be none other than Christ himself. How much greater is he than they? If he were only human, there would be some reasonable comparison; but he is Son of God, so there is none. The difference is absolute, though it is expressed comparatively.

Usually this idiom is quite clear, with the context giving the key in each case. We can see the point when we ask, How much greater? How much better? A little thought will then show us whether it is literal or idiomatic. Consider these references: 1 Samuel 15:22; Ezra 9:13; Psalm 118:8-9; Proverbs 21:3; Hebrews 1:4; 3:3; 6:9.

4. *Son of* or *daughter of.* This expression really covers several idioms:

a. A *son* is a *real descendant* but of a later generation— that is, a grandson or someone even further removed. The Hebrews used the verb *begat* in a similar way. It could refer to an actual son or to someone later in the line. The Hebrews did not forget who was the father of whom or write carelessly; they spoke or wrote using this idiom. This explains what otherwise seem to be mistakes. Matthew 1:8 says that Joram begat Uzziah, but 1 Chronicles 3:11-12 shows that three generations are omitted between the two names. (Azariah is the same as Uzziah.) Other references are 1 Kings 15:3; 1 Chronicles 26:24.

b. A person was called *the son of a quality* when he pos-
sessed that quality, perhaps with the idea of having his father's nature. In Acts 4:36 the apostles named a man *barnabas*
because he was what the name means: a *son of encouragement.*
(See also Job 41:34; Is. 14:12; Mt. 8:12; Lk. 10:6; Eph. 2:3;
5:6; 1 Thess. 5:5.)

c. *My son* shows affection and *your son* shows respect,
where there is no blood relationship. Consider 1 Samuel
24:16 and 25:8.

d. The nation is called *son* by God, as in Jeremiah 31:9.
There God says, "I am a father to Israel, and Ephraim is
my first-born." (See also Hos. 11:1.)

e. Citizens are called *sons of the nation.* Consider Lamentations 4:2 or Zechariah 9:13. The whole nation is called
daughter [or *virgin daughter*] *of Zion* (Lam. 2:13).

There is no great problem in interpreting these idioms.
When you understand the above possibilities, you can consider each verse in its context. The particular aspect of the
idiom is usually quite clear. This may not be as true in the
genealogies, and you may have to do some comparing with
other passages. In some cases it may be impossible to decide.

Remember, too, that in most passages when you read *son
of* it is not an idiom but a simple, literal statement. There are
also some special instances. *Sons of God* in Job 1:6 and 2:1,
and possibly in Genesis 6:2, 4, refers to angels. *Sons of men*
seems to mean "men" and *Son of man,* as in many verses in
Ezekiel (2:1; 3:1; 4:1), is also a phrase for "man." When
used of Christ in Daniel's prophecy, however, it speaks of
one who is more than human (Dan. 7:13).

We must also consider this special use of the phrase *son
of:* One of Jesus Christ's titles is *Son of God.* In at least one
passage (Lk. 1:30-35) the name is used in connection with
Jesus' birth as a child conceived through the power of the
Holy Spirit and born of a virgin mother. But in nearly all
New Testament passages the name denotes his eternal son-

ship, his having the same nature as God the Father. It does not mean that he is less than God but that he is truly God. Study these passages: John 10:33-36; 19:7; Hebrews 1:8.

Believers, too, are called *sons of God*. This indicates that believers are "partakers of the divine nature" (2 Pet. 1:4) and are destined to be glorified, like Christ (1 Jn. 3:2). They shall never become God; rather, they will always be his servants and forever worship him (Rev. 22:3).

5. *For ever*. Literally the word means *eternally* or *everlastingly*. Examples of its use in the literal sense are Psalm 9:7 ("the Lord sits enthroned for ever") and Psalm 45:6 ("Your divine throne endures for ever and ever").

It is also used idiomatically to mean "continuing without hindrance or interruption during the lifetime or existence of the subject referred to." Exodus 21:6 (AV) instructs that a servant who loves his master and wants to continue serving him rather than to go free in the seventh year (v. 2) should have his ear bored as a sign that "he shall serve him for ever." Since both master and servant will eventually die, the service will come to an end. *For ever* here means that the service cannot be stopped as long as both master and servant are alive. In fact, the RSV translates this "he shall serve him for life."

We can also see this in Psalm 72:17: "May his name endure for ever, his fame continue as long as the sun!" The second clause is parallel to the first, so the *for ever* in the first does not necessarily mean without end. The sun will come to an end, but nothing can hurt God's name or fame as long as his order continues.

This idiomatic use of the word *for ever* does not take all the meaning away. It retains tremendous meaning: What is for ever will last as long as the person or thing exists. Nothing can stop or interfere with it, especially when it is a promise or declaration of God. God's promises are sure. Nor does it raise a question about the realities that are truly endless, such as the Lord enduring for ever. However, to be accurate in our understanding of the Bible language we must recognize this idiom. Other references are 2 Kings 5:27; 2 Chronicles 7:16; Psalm 49:11; Isaiah 32:14-15; Jeremiah 31:35-36.

Guidelines for Interpretation

1. *Learn the various idioms and their possible uses.*

2. *Consider whether a passage can be a literal statement.* If that does not make sense, then consider the possibility that it contains an idiom.

3. *Examine the context.* Nearly always you will find a key for the interpretation.

The Bible has a number of other idioms we have not discussed. If possible, consult additional books to learn and understand them. Also, use your own careful study to identify more idioms.

18 Hebrew Poetry

Poetry is a means of expressing some of the deepest and highest thoughts and feelings of the human heart. We recognize poetry but probably cannot define it. It is a literary form which in English is marked by a definite structure of lines that have rhythm and often rhyme. Its language is usually beautiful and elevated.

The Bible contains a great deal of poetry: Not only Psalms and Proverbs but also Job, Song of Solomon, Lamentations and large parts of the prophets. Even some sayings of Jesus seem to be poetical. (See Mt. 7:6 and Jn. 6:35.) The AV does not indicate the poetical sections by printing them as poetry, so they are hard to recognize, except for Psalms and Proverbs. The RSV and other recent versions print the poetry in poetical form.

Features of Poetry
The features of Bible poetry are clear in the Hebrew, but some of them are lost in translation. In order to aid interpretation, we need to be able to recognize those which show up in our versions.

1. *Parallelism.* The main feature of Hebrew poetry is a rhythm of thought (rather than of sound) called *parallelism*. This means simply that the poetry is written in couplets, two

lines that are related to each other in some way. Occasionally there are three lines (Is. 41:5) or even four (Ps. 27:1), but usually two. For example,

Wash me thoroughly from my iniquity,

and cleanse me from my sin! (Ps. 51:2)

The relation of the two lines to each other is not always the same. In fact we can speak of different kinds of parallelism to express different basic ideas. Each of these has its proper name.

a. *Repetition,* expressed by *identical, or synonymous, parallelism.* The two lines express the same or similar thought in different words. Isaiah 1:3 has a good example:

Israel does not know,

my people does not understand.

The second line repeats the same thought for clarity or emphasis. Psalm 33:2 is similar in form:

Praise the LORD with the lyre,

make melody to him with the harp of ten strings.

Here is the same general idea, but the instrument and act are different.

In this parallelism one line often throws light on the other one (again, the principle of context). In Isaiah 45:7 (AV) the first line establishes *light* and *darkness* as opposites. So *peace* and *evil* in the second line are doubtlessly opposites, too. If so, then the evil is not moral evil but confusion or chaos. The verse does not say that God is the author of sin. (Note the RSV.)

b. *Contrast,* expressed by *antithetic parallelism.* To make the truth more emphatic and forceful, the two lines express contrasting, or even contradictory, thoughts. Proverbs has a great deal of this kind of parallelism. Often the second line of a couplet starts with *but,* indicating a contrast. Proverbs 15:1,

A soft answer turns away wrath,

but a harsh word stirs up anger.

(See also Prov. 10, where each of the first fourteen verses

is antithetic parallelism.)

c. *Addition,* expressed by *synthetic parallelism.* In this, the second line adds a complementary thought to the first. Sometimes it gives the reason for the first, beginning with the word *for.* (See Ps. 9:10.) Or it may show purpose, beginning with *that* or *so that.* (See Ps. 104:5.) Some students say this is not true parallelism, yet because there are related lines and a balanced construction, I think we may consider it as such.

d. *Expansion,* expressed in *climactic parallelism.* The second line repeats part of the first but adds something fresh— a new step, as it were. Psalm 34:4,

I sought the Lord, and he answered me,
and delivered me from all my fears.

What part of the first line is expanded in the second?

e. *Transformation,* expressed by *emblematic parallelism.* Emblematic means symbolic or representing. One line is literal while the other is figurative. Since commonly the two lines are talking about the same thing, it is usually also synonymous parallelism. In one form you will recognize a simile, for example, Psalm 42:1,

As a hart longs for flowing streams,
so longs my soul for thee, O God.

The simile of the thirsty deer adds beauty and vividness to the psalmist's statement about his desire for God. The form may also be metaphoric, as in Isaiah 46:11, which speaks of "calling a bird of prey from the east, the man of my counsel from a far country." In effect, God says the man of his counsel is a bird of prey. Our knowledge of the use of parallelism helps us understand that *bird of prey* is not literal.

You will find many places where the lines do not seem to fit any of the patterns we have seen. Do not worry if you find it hard to name the pattern. Often the meaning will be quite clear (for example, Ps. 47:4, 9).

There are many varieties of parallelism and not all are clear. Some lines have incomplete thought or structure.

The biblical writers were not mechanical in their writing of poetry. Often they joined two or more couplets in combined parallelism. As you study the poetry, you can find examples of the various forms.

How do we interpret the parallelism? When we know that lines of poetry are related we will not take each one in isolation but will seek to find the relationship. We also know some of the possible relationships so if we have doubts about the meaning we can try different possibilities to see which one fits best.

Let us see how this works with an example, Psalm 22:16:

Yes, dogs are round about me;

a company of evildoers encircle me;

they have pierced my hands and feet.

It is possible, though rather strange, that the psalmist should be surrounded by a pack of real dogs. If it is emblematic parallelism, *dogs* may be figurative for the *evildoers* of the second line. As we read the whole psalm (the context of this verse), we see other figures, including mention of other animals (as in v. 6, "I am a worm"); and this indicates emblematic parallelism in this verse.

Study also Psalm 60:3, in which the drinking of wine may be either literal or figurative. Considering it as emblematic parallelism avoids the meaning that God made his people drunk with alcohol. Other figures in the psalm also suggest that this line is probably figurative.

2. *Imagery.* All poetry has much figurative language in it —beautiful, striking, bold pictures. We find the various figures of speech in Bible poetry. We have already considered how to interpret them.

3. *Hyperbolic language.* The hyperbole is a figure of speech, but its use in poetry is so significant that we need to consider it separately. Poetry often expresses strong emotion, and the poet seems driven to use extravagant language to express his intense feeling. If we do not recognize such statements, we will find it hard to understand some pas-

sages of Scripture.

Job provides an example of this. In 6:26 he appeals to his friends to recognize that "the speech of a despairing man is wind." He knows his words will be extravagant. He speaks such wild words in 16:12-13, saying that God "seized me by the neck and dashed me to pieces . . . he slashes open my kidneys." He is not speaking literally, as chapters 1 and 2 show, but is giving vent to his deep and strong feeling. We can understand his speech in that way. You will find numbers of such instances in the Psalms, Lamentations and Jeremiah.

A special aspect of this kind of language is found in what are called the Imprecatory Psalms, the psalms in which the writer calls for the curse or judgment of God upon enemies. Some of the main references are Psalms 58:6-11; 59:5, 13; 69:22-23; 109:6-15; 137:8-9; 139:19-22; 143:12.

These passages give us a significant problem of interpretation, for the attitude they express seems to be contrary to God's merciful, loving attitude toward sinners. If we say that the writers are honestly stating their own thoughts but that those thoughts are not in line with God's will and purpose, then we will be in much uncertainty, not knowing what else in the Psalms is only of man and not of God. This problem has no simple answer. We have to consider the passages carefully, especially in the light of the background which is often indicated in the heading to the psalm. Here are some points which may help:

a. *Some of the harsh expressions are figurative, not meant to be taken literally.* Just as Job spoke harshly of God, so the psalmist uses such language: "let their eyes be darkened," "break the teeth in their mouths," "the righteous . . . will bathe his feet in the blood of the wicked," "happy shall he be who takes your little ones and dashes them against the rock." It would be as unfair to take these literally as to take Job in that way. The writers are expressing their love for God and their deep concern for his honor, truth and holiness which is being defiled by those who rebel against him and spurn his mercy. Intense feeling brings forth violent language. Perhaps one reason we find it hard to understand is that we know little of that intense jealousy for God that the psalm writers had.

b. *The writers are speaking not only of their own personal enemies but of those who are enemies of God.* In other words, it is not just a personal quarrel. In Psalm 139 this point is especially clear: The writer says he hates the wicked because they defy God. You can see expressions that are somewhat similar in the New Testament, even some words of Christ: Matthew 18:5-6; 1 Corinthians 16:22; Galatians 1:8-9; Revelation 6:10; 18:20.

c. *Note the difference between David's writing about his enemies, including Saul, and his actual treatment of Saul.* In Psalm 18:40 he wrote, "those who hated me I destroyed." Notice the heading of the psalm. In 1 Samuel 24:1-7 and 26:1-11, we see that he twice treated Saul in a patient and restrained manner; he refused to harm him. This comparison of Scripture with Scripture helps to confirm that the language is hyperbolic.

The poetry of the Bible speaks to our hearts very personally because it comes from sinful men like us—men needing and conscious of God's grace—who are pouring out their hearts before God in deep feelings of shame, love, gratitude and devotion. As much as from any part of the Bible, in poetry we can see ourselves and learn to see God.

Guidelines for Interpretation

1 *Analyze the lines of each couplet to see how they are related to each other.* Check each one with the list of various kinds of parallelism. Look for synonyms or antonyms and key words like *but* and *that*. Look for indications of whether one line is figurative, the other literal.

2. *Look for figures of speech.* Analyze and interpret them according to the principles suggested in Chapter 13.

3. *Consider all extreme, harsh or violent language in light of the fact that poetry uses such language as prose does not.* Remember that such language may express the deep feeling of the writer toward God's enemies, not just toward his own.

19   Prophecy

One writer has said that in the study of prophecy the Bible student finds some of the greatest problems of interpretation. This may well be true, but it need not make us fearful or discouraged. We recognize that there is a great difference of conviction about Bible prophecy, yet prophecy, especially the predictions about Christ's first and second coming, is one of the most important parts of the Bible. We must exert all the effort we can to learn what God has made known about the future.

In the original and primary meaning a prophet is a spokesman, one who speaks for another. Note Exodus 4:16 and 7:1 where Aaron is said to be Moses' prophet, speaking Moses' message. God's prophet, then, is one who speaks for God, giving God's message. He speaks to men mainly concerning the present; he may or may not speak about the future. Because prediction is the more common meaning of prophecy, we will use the word prophecy in that way in considering its interpretation. We will seek to understand the biblical statements through which God revealed the future.

A fairly large part of the Bible consists of future predictions. Found in both Old and New Testaments, they are of various kinds:

1. *Immediate predictions.* Those fulfilled a short time after

being uttered. Exodus 14:4, 13-17; Jeremiah 38:18.

2. *Old Testament predictions fulfilled later in Old Testament times.* Deuteronomy 28:53 and Lamentations 4:10; Joshua 6:26 and 1 Kings 16:34.

3. *Old Testament prophecies fulfilled in New Testament times.* These concern especially those fulfilled in Christ's person and ministry. They are the main part of the subject of prophecy and the ones we will chiefly consider. References are numerous.

4. *New Testament prophecies fulfilled in New Testament times.* Matthew 16:21 and Matthew 27.

5. *Unfulfilled Old Testament and New Testament prophecies.* These relate mainly to the second coming of Christ. We shall consider them in depth also.

Some of these groupings overlap. For example, some Old Testament prophecies have to do with both comings of Christ. And some New Testament prophecies concerning both the present period and the second coming are as yet unfulfilled.

We should note that prophecy includes more than specific predictions, such as 1 Timothy 4:1. Types are another part of the prophetic portion of Scripture. Visions are a special way in which God gave the prophetic message. A vision had to be interpreted even to the prophet himself. Daniel 4 and Revelation 17 are good examples.

Characteristics of Prophecy

To interpret Bible prophecy we need to understand its main characteristics.

1. *Prophetic perspective.* This means the prophet's point of view. He was, so to speak, looking spiritually into the distance, seeing various future events as God revealed them to him. His experience was similar to looking at the Himalayan mountains from a long distance. A person sees several peaks, and from his vantage point they seem to be close together. If he goes near them, however, he sees that they are

far apart. Likewise the prophets saw two great "peaks"—the first and second comings of Christ, his suffering and triumph—and spoke of them together, as if they are close in time. They are logically close, yet in time they are far apart, as we now know.

Consider Isaiah 61:1-3, for example. Christ referred this to himself by reading part of it and then saying the Scripture was fulfilled that very day (Lk. 4:16-21). In Isaiah 61:2, however, two great proclamations were predicted. One was the year of grace and the other the day of vengeance. Christ read the first but stopped before the second. Why? What period does the day of vengeance refer to? Certainly not to his first coming. This portion was not fulfilled then, so he did not read it. In the prophecy, however, the two realities are put close together. You can find similar passages, like Genesis 3:15 and Psalm 22.

2. *Near and far fulfillment.* Many prophecies referred first of all to an event near the time of the prophecy, but, because God is the Lord of all history, he ordained that the prophecy have a later and final fulfillment as well. Thus the first fulfillment is typical of the second. An example of this feature of prophecy is 2 Samuel 7:12-16, the Lord's promise to David concerning his son. The prophecy clearly refers to Solomon, who succeeded David on the throne, and some details, like verse 14b, can refer only to Solomon. In Hebrews 1:5, verse 14 is also applied to Christ: He is David's greater Son and Solomon is typical of him. Solomon was a son of David and a son of God. So was Christ, though with a profound difference.

Habakkuk 1:5-6 and Acts 13:41 is another instance where we have New Testament authority for seeing a double fulfillment. When we have such authority, we can be sure of the interpretation. Without it we should not be dogmatic.

One prophecy that seems to show this feature but still is difficult to interpret is Isaiah's prophecy of Christ's virgin birth (Is. 7:14). When Ahaz did not respond to God's word, God said he would give the king a sign, a child born of a virgin. The context (especially vv. 16-17) indicates that the prophecy was fulfilled at that time; therefore, the child must have been born then. But Matthew applies the prophecy to Christ (Mt. 1:22-23). This raises a major problem: Was there an actual virgin birth at the time of Ahaz? There is no evidence that there was. Perhaps a young woman who was a virgin at the time of the prophecy was then married and had a son within a short time. There is also some question about the meaning of the Hebrew word translated *virgin*. There is no question about Matthew 1:23, however: The context confirms that the word there means only a virgin. This prophecy is difficult, and Bible students do not agree on the interpretation, but the reference to Christ and the double fulfillment are clear.

3. *Figurative language.* Prophecies have a great many figures of speech, symbols, etc., which we have already considered. They also have literal statements. The problem of interpretation is not just the individual figures but the larger question of whether prophecy is fulfilled literally, or in a figurative or spiritual way. Our approach to this question is based upon the premise that fulfilled prophecy is the key to understanding the unfulfilled. We must see how the New Testament interprets Old Testament prophecies. It will be well to look at several of these.

a. *Aren't the following prophecies fulfilled literally, according to the New Testament?*

Micah 5:2 and Matthew 2:6: Christ's birthplace, Bethlehem.

Zechariah 9:9 and Matthew 21:5: Christ entering Jerusalem as king, riding on a donkey.

Isaiah 56:7 and Matthew 21:13: God's house, the literal temple, a house of prayer.

Isaiah 7:14 and Matthew 1:22-23: A virgin bears a son.

Psalm 22:18 and John 19:23-24: Soldiers divide Christ's

garments and cast lots.

b. *Aren't the following prophecies fulfilled in a figurative way?*

Psalm 118:22 and Acts 4:11; 1 Peter 2:7: Christ, the stone rejected by builders.

Isaiah 22:22 and Revelation 3:7: The key on his shoulder suggests his kingly authority.

Zechariah 13:7 and Matthew 26:31: Christ, the shepherd who was smitten.

c. *Aren't the following prophecies fulfilled in a spiritual way, a literal Old Testament reality prefiguring a spiritual New Testament one?*

Jeremiah 31:31-34 and Hebrews 8:8-12; 10:15-17: The new covenant with Israel, the spiritual experience of Gentile believers now.

Isaiah 2:2-3 and Hebrews 12:22: The earthly Zion and Jerusalem speak of the spiritual abode of believers.

Amos 9:11-12 and Acts 15:16-17: The booth of David and Edom are now fulfilled spiritually.

If the New Testament interprets prophecies in these three different ways, then it seems plain that we may interpret other prophecies in any one of the three. This does not help us to know quickly or easily what is the right interpretation, but it does help us to know the possibilities. God shows us that all prophecies are not to be interpreted in the same way. And the more we study the New Testament treatment of prophecies, the more we will have insight into the understanding of all prophecies. We will later consider some guidelines.

4. *Special grammar.* This may not be the best title for this characteristic of prophecy, because prophecies normally use the same grammar as other parts of Scripture; but at times prophecy has special ways of using tenses.

a. *Verbs in the past tense may be used for future events.* The great prophecy of Christ in Isaiah 53 is, up to verse 10a, in the past tense, though it foretells the future. Verses 10b-12 are in the future tense (speaking of what was to follow the suffering of Christ), though they are no more future to the time of the prophecy than the first part.

b. *Present tense may be used for the future.* In Zechariah 9:9 *your king comes to you* is in the present tense, but it looks to the future.

5. *Conditional and unconditional predictions.* While many prophecies are unconditional—that is, God declares what he will do or what will come to pass regardless of other factors—the fulfillment of many others depends on the response of people. Commonly, conditional predictions are general predictions of either blessing or judgment, rather than foretellings of definite events. They are nonetheless true prophecies, and the Bible records the fulfillment of many of them. Some passages are Deuteronomy 28; Jeremiah 18:8, 10; 26:12-13; Ezekiel 18:30-32; 33:13-15; John 3:4 (can tell from the context). The context of all prophecies is important, for if there is a condition, it may be there.

6. *Revealing and hiding truth.* Some people think that prophecy is simply history written in advance. Because prophecies do provide some remarkable details at times, people conclude that prophecy is intended to disclose practically all facts. But many prophecies hide the truth as well as reveal it. Representative is Daniel's vision of four beasts (Dan. 7). In 7:15-16 Daniel says that he was troubled by it and asked a figure in his vision about the meaning. He says further that the figure made known to him the interpretation: He was told that the beasts represent four kings or kingdoms. He was not informed, however, about the name of the kingdoms nor some of the details. So it would have been impossible for him to know in advance who the kings would be. Truth was revealed but also concealed in the vision. So we should exercise caution in thinking that we can interpret unfulfilled prophecies with complete certainty.

A Key Prophecy

The above features of biblical prophecies are important for

us to remember. They become some of the guidelines for interpreting the prophecies we study.

It will help us to apply them to one of the most important Old Testament prophecies: the first direct prophecy of Christ in the Bible, Genesis 3:15. We can see that this one exhibits several of the features we have noticed and, in addition, contains central themes of prophecy that we find throughout the Word of God.

1. *Prophetic perspective.* What future events are predicted by the bruising of the seed's heel and of the serpent's head? Though these are put together, Jesus' suffering and triumph, including his two comings, are the fulfillment.

2. *Near and far fulfillment.* The enmity that God put between the woman and the serpent had near fulfillment in the life of Eve. Its far fulfillment was the conflict between Christ and Satan.

3. *Figurative language.* Bruising the head and heel cannot be literal; they have a fullness of spiritual meaning far beyond a physical hurt.

4. *Revealing and hiding truth.* Some truth is revealed, but the full meaning of the prophecy can be understood only in the light provided by later prophecies and events.

5. *The theme of conflict.* The whole Bible is concerned with this conflict: God versus Satan; God's people versus the devil's agents. Christ, as the seed of woman, entered history to win the conflict.

6. *The theme of God's sovereign purpose.* "I will put," God says. Throughout the Bible God's purpose is being worked out, though at times it seems that Satan is on top. The book of Revelation shows the ultimate working out of that purpose.

7. *The theme of the Messiah.* The *seed of the woman* and the pronoun *he* shows that an individual person is in view.

8. *The theme of Messiah's suffering.* "You shall bruise his heel." Such a wound is not necessarily fatal, but does picture suffering.

9. *The theme of Messiah's triumph.* That "he shall bruise your head" indicates the fatal wound that the Messiah will give the serpent, Satan. The picture suggests comparison, wounding in the heel or in the head.

The last two themes are the central themes of prophecy. Peter summed up the message of the prophets as "the sufferings of Christ and the subsequent glory" (1 Pet. 1:11). Jesus reproached the two disciples for not believing what the prophets had written of him, that "the Christ should suffer these things and enter into his glory" (Lk. 24:25-26). The suffering and glory of Christ are the two focal points of Old Testament prophecy. All other points and themes find their meaning in relation to them.

Guidelines for Interpretation

It will help if we summarize the guidelines for the interpretation of prophecy.

1. *Study the New Testament treatment of prophecy.* This you should do even in your regular study of the New Testament, not only when you are trying to interpret one prophetic passage. Keep a notebook to record the passages and what you have learned in your study of them.

2. *In each prophecy seek to understand first its meaning for the people at that time, its near fulfillment and its practical message.* It is important to learn this before trying to find a future fulfillment. For example, the book of Haggai has to do with building God's house. What can that mean? Ezra 4:24—5:2 provides the background and shows the aim of Haggai's speaking. His exhortation to build God's house is linked with his prediction of what God will do in the future to show his divine power in heaven and earth and to bless his people. Hebrews 12:26-29 brings out the far fulfillment.

3. *Consider the literal meaning.* Is the meaning clear, without difficulty from the context or from other Scripture? Isaiah 11:6-9 gives a beautiful picture of harmony in the future. Is there anything impossible about wild animals living

together with domestic ones and with little children? Could this have a literal fulfillment? Do you notice indications of figurative language in the passage? (See vv. 1, 4-5.) Could the language in those verses indicate a possible figurative meaning for verses 6-9?

4. *Keep in mind the features of prophecy we have considered.* Seek to recognize any that may be in the passage. If you find them, interpret accordingly. For instance, in John 5:28-29 is a prophecy of the resurrection from the dead. Or does it foretell two resurrections? The language could be understood either way. Remembering that sometimes in prophetic perspective events separated in time may be joined in one prophecy, you realize that the two resurrections mentioned might be separated in time (not that they *must* be, but that they *might* be). You will have to study other passages to see if they are or not.

5. *Look for figures of speech, symbols, idioms, etc., in the passages.* If you find them, seek to interpret by the guidelines for these. You must observe carefully, for some figures are so common that we hardly notice them.

Prophecy is not an easy subject, but it is one of God's channels for teaching us blessed truth. It pays to give much study and prayer to this important area of God's revelation.

20 Doctrine

The word *doctrine* is used in two ways: (1) to refer to truth as a whole, a system of truth, and (2) to refer to a particular truth. Bible doctrine in sense (1) is God's overall teaching. A Bible doctrine in sense (2) is one element of God's truth, such as the second coming of Christ. Scripture is the basis for both. So, in order to formulate correct doctrine, we must understand the meaning of Scripture. This again emphasizes the importance of diligent Bible study and accurate interpretation.

The Bible, unlike a textbook, does not treat doctrines one at a time. One reason for this is that doctrine is not a branch of knowledge to be learned for its own sake. Rather, it is truth for living. We learn about God in order that we may live in fellowship with him and in obedience to his will. Paul says that "all Scripture . . . is profitable for doctrine . . . that the man of God may be . . ." (2 Tim. 3:16). God gave the Scripture so that we can be what he wants us to be.

We can see the point in such passages as 1 John 3:2-3: "When he appears we shall be like him. . . . And every one who thus hopes in him purifies himself as he is pure." Our belief in the second coming should lead to purity of life. (See also great doctrinal passages like Is. 40:27-31 and Phil. 2:5-8.)

The Bible, therefore, gives the truth of God in life situations. We learn doctrine through Abraham's life, through David's struggles, through the prophets' appeals to Israel. Even the doctrinal epistles in the New Testament are letters written to people to help them live as Christians. So we can expect to find a truth taught in a number of places. For the doctrine of God hundreds or perhaps even thousands of verses are relevant.

Approach to Doctrine

It is well to set down plainly our approach to the study of doctrine in Scripture. What are the convictions with which we start?

1. *The Bible gives us the doctrine God wants us to know.* 2 Timothy 3:16-17 makes this clear. All Scripture is profitable for doctrine.

2. *The Bible is a sufficient source of doctrine.* God has given us in this one book all the doctrine we need to know. There is no other authoritative source. Neither church tradition nor our own reason nor intuition nor anything else outside the Bible is adequate to teach God's truth.

3. *The Bible gives a unified presentation of doctrine.* The doctrine taught in the New Testament does not contradict that taught in the Old. Paul does not contradict Jesus, nor James contradict Paul. The Bible is a clear and consistent revelation of God's truth.

There may be, however, different emphases in different parts of the Bible. Jeremiah emphasizes God's judgment on the sin of his people, while Hosea speaks more of God's mercy. But we cannot say, for instance, that the Old Testament teaches God's wrath and the New Testament his love. Both Testaments teach both the love and the wrath of God.

Still, the revelation of God's truth is progressive; that is, the earlier parts of the Bible do not give the fullness of truth. God revealed more and more of himself and his ways as time went on. The New Testament is the culmination and climax of God's revelation and is different from the Old. (We will consider this more in Chapter 21.)

4. *We are to learn doctrine by studying all the passages that touch on a particular subject.* Since our question is What does the Bible say? we study the whole of it to find out. We do not bring our own ideas to have the Bible confirm them. Nor do we form our doctrine from just one or two passages. This is a big task, which we will discuss more in a moment.

5. *We cannot expect to understand everything about God.* We are creatures; he is the infinite Creator. Because he is infinitely above us, our minds cannot take in all the truth about him. Therefore, we expect to find in the Bible things difficult to understand and questions that we cannot answer. While we accept and seek to live by what we can understand, we trust God for what is beyond our comprehension.

6. *We expect to find paradoxical truth in the Bible.* A paradox means that some phases of truth seem to be opposites, yet both are taught in the Bible. We cannot seem to fit them together logically. For example, the Bible teaches that Christ is both God and man. God is unlimited; man is limited. So how can Christ be both unlimited and limited at the same time? Yet he is, according to what the Bible teaches. Scholars cannot solve all the problems that arise, but they, and we, must accept the Bible's teaching and hold both truths as aspects of the doctrine of Christ.

7. *Doctrine is meant to produce godliness.* As we study the doctrines, we will seek to understand and obey God's message.

Guidelines for Interpretation
Now let us consider how we can learn doctrine from our study of the Bible.

1. *Base doctrine on the literal statements of the Bible rather than on the figurative portions.* Figurative passages (such as parables) are given to teach a main lesson. We might easily find doctrine in some details that are just part of the story

and not meant to teach doctrine. Also, interpreting a "picture" is more problematic than interpreting a plain statement.

For example, consider the parable of the Prodigal Son (Lk. 15). Some liberal theologians take this as teaching the way a sinner can get back to God. And since there is no atoning death in the story, they conclude that God is a loving father who only requires that a sinner repent. Christ's suffering the punishment for sin is unnecessary, they say.

Or consider the allegory of the vine and the branches (Jn. 15). In this picture some branches are burned. Do they represent true believers? Can true believers be burned up in the end? If so, in what sense? The answers to these questions should be found in plain statements; then this passage may illustrate the truth. We are unwise to formulate doctrine from this passage.

2. *Base doctrine on plain statements rather than on obscure ones.* The Bible does have obscure passages. Some passages may seem plain to one student and hard to another. Nevertheless, some passages are recognized as difficult by all students, and it is wise not to base doctrine on them.

For example, Peter says that Jesus "went and preached to the spirits in prison" (1 Pet. 3:19). Bible scholars do not agree on the meaning of this difficult verse. So it would be unwise to conclude from it that a sinner will have another chance for repentance after his death. Plain passages state that there is no second chance.

3. *Base doctrine on the didactic (teaching) passages rather than on the historical ones.* A good deal of the prophetic books and practically all of the discourses of Christ and the epistles are didactic. By definition, teaching portions give teaching. Historical portions record events, so the teaching in them is more indirect and implied. Of course, sometimes during an event God or one of his prophets did speak, but we should not base doctrine merely on the implications of someone's actions.

For example, Jesus was once asleep in a boat during a storm, and the disciples were afraid (Mt. 8:24). Shall we be so silly as to conclude that God is unaware of or does not care about our danger? In Matthew 25:5 the ten virgins all slumbered. Does that mean that everyone will be sleeping when Jesus comes back? Again, we should be cautious about forming the doctrine of the Holy Spirit simply from the events recorded in Acts. We learn from them, but we must have the Spirit-given teaching of the epistles to be sure we have the doctrine clear.

4. *Base doctrine on all the relevant passages, not on just a few.* It is wrong to look at a small number of passages, form a doctrine from them and then try to interpret other passages to agree with this doctrine. The other passages should be considered from the beginning.

For example, suppose a Christian looks at 1 Thessalonians 1:10 and 5:9, which say that "Jesus who delivers us from the wrath to come" and "God has not destined us for wrath." He decides from these verses alone that God will not let the church go through what is called *The Great Tribulation* at the end time. If he concludes that without looking at other passages, such as Matthew 24:29-51, it will not be a fair way to treat the Scripture nor to arrive at correct doctrine.

The problem, of course, is that for some doctrines there are hundreds of passages. It takes a long time to go through the Bible to find them, let alone to study them all thoroughly. It may, then, be impossible for you to do this. But you should seek to do at least some doctrinal study in this way, for it will help greatly in your understanding of God's truth.

We recognize that all cannot do such extensive study. So many will have to learn doctrine from teachers in the church, either through books or sermons or Bible studies. This may well be the area in which the teachers whom God has put in the church can make the greatest contribution. God does give to some the gifts that are needed for this ministry: to learn the truth, formulate it clearly and communicate it to believers. Do not be disappointed if you are not able to acquire all of your doctrinal knowledge by your study alone.

5. *Do a word study to learn some doctrines.* Do this particularly when the doctrine is summed up in one biblical word, such as *Sabbath.* Use a concordance. You can do word study without a concordance, but it is more difficult. And remember these points:

a. *There are doctrines which have no one word in the Bible to describe them.* Consequently, no word study can be made for them—for example, the word *Trinity.*

b. *There are passages in which a doctrine is presented but the actual word does not occur.* In studying a doctrine we do not want to ignore such passages. For example, the word *sanctification* is found in 1 Thessalonians 4:3; however, in 1 John 1 and 3 the doctrine is discussed but the word is not used. Those passages have important bearing on the doctrine nonetheless.

c. *Some doctrines have more than one word to express them.* Do not study one word and ignore the others. For instance, *sanctification, holiness* and *purification* are words related to one doctrine.

6. *Be sure that each passage is understood through the general principles of interpretation.* We can never get away from the basic guidelines for all interpretation. For example, in studying *sanctification* the tense of the verb is important in verses such as 1 John 3:6, 9, as we have seen.

7. *Be cautious in formulating doctrine by inference.* Suppose a certain truth is taught in one passage of Scripture. We conclude that if it is true then something else follows from it. This "something else" is an inference. We do not find it clearly stated in the Bible but derive it from a truth we do find in Scripture. We must remember that it is an inference and, if we teach it, teach it as such.

For example, some Bible students see God's sovereign

election of some individuals to be taught plainly in Scripture. So they infer from that that God must have elected other people to damnation. But that is an inference. The Bible nowhere says this. Such an inference may or may not be true; even if it were, we would still have to consider it an inference.

8. *Beware of doctrinal speculation.* Often in meditating on Scripture our mind starts considering possibilities and it is easy to speculate. We may think of some people being as babies and others as adults in the eternal state. We may think of our inhabiting other planets in the future ages. Right or wrong, these are speculations, not taught in the Bible. We must beware of them.

9. *In forming, holding and teaching doctrine, emphasize what the Scripture emphasizes.* All truth that God has revealed is important, but some truths are more important than others. The truth that Christ is coming back again is more important than the question of whether the church will be on earth during the period of suffering known as *The Great Tribulation.* Paul indicates in 1 Corinthians 1:17 that he recognized priorities in his ministry, suggesting priorities in doctrine, too. So seek not simply to understand the doctrines but also to see which truths the Bible lays the emphasis on.

10. *Seek the practical import of the doctrine.* Normally the Bible will state that practical point since God has revealed the truth for that reason. It is our duty both to find it and to seek God's enabling to carry it out.

The Doctrine of the Trinity

It will help us to consider one important doctrine of Scripture to see both how we can learn doctrine and also some of the problems of such study. We will consider briefly the doctrine of the Trinity.

This doctrine, and even the word itself, has come into the Christian faith as devoted Bible students have observed certain lines of truth given in the Bible:

1. *There is one God:* Deuteronomy 6:4; 1 Timothy 2:5; and other verses.

2. *There is a divine being called the "Father," who is God:* Romans 1:7; Ephesians 4:6; Philippians 2:11.

3. *There is another divine being, called "Jesus Christ the Son of God,"* who is God: John 5:18; Hebrews 1:8; 2 Peter 1:1; 1 John 4:15.

4. *There is another divine being, called the "Holy Spirit," who is God:* Acts 5:3-4.

5. *There are distinctions among these three divine beings,* which show personal differences:

Matthew 3:16: Jesus, the Spirit as a dove, the voice from heaven.

John 14:26: The Father will send the Counselor.

John 15:26: Jesus will send the Counselor, who will bear witness.

John 5:20: The Father loves the Son.

How can the five biblical truths be combined? Three are said to be God, yet there is only one God. The three are distinct from each other so they cannot be only qualities, aspects or modes of one being. The truth, therefore, must be that in one God there are three Persons. The word *Person* does not really explain or describe them, but, since the distinctions are personal, *Person* seems the best word to use. We can easily see that in speaking of doctrines relating to God, words are often inadequate. We are dealing with revealed truth, which we cannot fully comprehend. Yet we accept it, and the church of Christ through the centuries has accepted it, as true doctrine. It is confirmed in other passages, such as Matthew 28:19; 2 Corinthians 13:14; Revelation 1:4-5.

Your living according to God's will depends on your growing in the knowledge of him so you should do some doctrinal study as you seek to understand your Bible. It will take work, but you will reap rich spiritual rewards.

21 The Relation of the Old and New Testaments

In seeking to understand the Bible, Christians, especially young ones, find the meaning of the Old Testament and its relation to the New one of their biggest problems. For many Christians the Old Testament is confusing, so they give up trying to understand it. They do nearly all their reading in the New Testament, except perhaps for the Psalms.

But this is neither good nor necessary. God has given us one Bible, which includes both Testaments. The Old Testament is his Word to us, and we can understand it. Christ once explained the Old Testament to two disciples (Lk. 24), and the Holy Spirit can explain it to us today. How then shall we study it?

Points of Unity

The natural way to grasp the meaning of the Old Testament is to see the way the New Testament looks at it. This is, so to speak, God's view of the relation of the two Testaments. So what is the New Testament's view of the Old? We can find answers to this question in a number of passages.

1. *God the Author.* According to Hebrews 1:1-3, God spoke to the fathers by the prophets. Since the writings of the prophets are found in the Old Testament, the Old Testament is from God. 2 Timothy 3:14-17 declares that "all

Scripture is inspired by God." When we think of what Scripture Timothy knew as a child, and what therefore is described in these verses, we realize that it is the Old Testament, for at that time the New Testament had not been collected and recognized as the Word of God. So these two passages both declare that God is the source of the Old Testament, and this is the view held consistently throughout the whole New Testament. You may want to consider other passages: Acts 28:23; Romans 1:17; 9:25; 2 Corinthians 6:2, 16.

2. *One Plan of Redemption.* The New Testament has more to say about the Old than simply that it is from God. Let us consider again 2 Timothy 3:14-17. What does Paul say is the value of the Old Testament? These holy writings, he teaches, are able to do something wonderful: Through them we can be instructed "for salvation" (v. 15). In other words, they show God's plan of redemption; they make known how man can be saved from sin.

What do other passages say? In Romans 4:1-9 Paul speaks of the spiritual experience of both Abraham and David. What was true of both of them? And what is the relation between their redemption and ours? God, Paul says, reckoned them righteous apart from works; they were justified by faith, or *by* grace *through* faith. So it is with us. It is on the same basis that both they and we get redemption. So this passage tells the same truth as the one in Timothy. In the Old Testament period, and through the Old Testament revelation, men knew God's plan of redemption. You can study other New Testament passages on this subject: Acts 24:14-15; Romans 4:10-25; 8:1-3; 11:13-24; Galatians 3:6-29; James 2:18-26.

The Old Testament tells us more than just how to be saved. It also teaches us about the walk with God. (See 2 Tim. 3:16-17; 1 Cor. 10:6, 11.) It contains much important spiritual truth to guide us in our daily lives.

3. *Christ the Center.* The New Testament says something

else about the Old Testament—something that surprises many people. Who is revealed in the Old Testament? The Old Testament not only gives a message of redemption, but it centers in the Person of Christ. Written before Christ came, of course, it still reveals him. Therefore, we are to read the Old Testament to see Christ, who appears in several ways.

a. *In certain great works.* One of them is the creation of the universe. Christ's name does not appear in Genesis 1, but what is the force of John 1:1-3; Colossians 1:16; and Hebrews 1:2? We may not know exactly how Christ participated in the creation, but this fact is clear: "all things were created through him." So when we read Old Testament passages about the creation, we should see Christ in them.

We can also think of other works Christ is doing. For instance, "in him all things hold together" (Col. 1:17). This work is called *providence* and includes sustaining the physical things of the world.

b. *In actual appearances.* These are called *theophanies,* which means "appearances of God." During Old Testament times God appeared in human form a number of times. There is evidence to suggest that when God appeared that way it was actually Christ. This does not mean that Christ became a true human being at that time, but rather that he assumed a human body (at least the form of a human body) for the purpose of the appearance.

We can look at Genesis 16 for one example. "The angel of the Lord" appears to Hagar (v. 7) and his authority is clear (v. 10). Hagar recognizes who this Person is (v. 13). In a number of passages *the* angel of the Lord is divine, while *an* angel is not. (See Gen. 22:11-12; 31:11-13.)

We can see that this Person is God, but why should we think that he is actually Christ? For one reason: Christ is the revelation of God. Many passages teach this. So we should expect that when God revealed himself in personal appearances it was Christ who appeared.

c. *In the national redemption of Israel.* This was one of the mighty works of God, referred to afterward as a great evidence of God's power (Deut. 6:12; 7:8; Judg. 6:8-10; Ps. 81:10; Jer. 23:7). The nation was redeemed from slavery in Egypt, brought through the wilderness and settled in the promised land. Paul refers to part of that history of redemption in 1 Corinthians 10:1-11. Those events have much to teach us just from the way God dealt with the people (v. 11), but Paul also indicates that Christ was present in the history (v. 4). The deeper meaning of the history concerns Christ: We can see him in the redemptive work, which is a great picture of his redemptive work for us.

d. *In personal redemption.* Through the Old Testament period God was dealing with individuals, seeking to bring them to faith and obedience. Many came to know God personally. Abraham, David and many other men and women lived by faith in God (Heb. 11). They were spiritually redeemed, and such redemption comes only by the work of Christ. Though they did not have the full historical revelation, those whose minds were open to understand the Scriptures had some knowledge from God concerning the death and resurrection of Christ and concerning redemption from sin (Lk. 24:45-47). The principle of atonement for sin was declared by God, pictured in sacrifice and anticipated in prophecy. The spiritually enlightened saw Christ's day and had some conception of his work (Jn. 8:56). They learned to know and walk with God (Gen. 5:22; 6:9; Job 19:25). Hebrews 11 makes clear that while there are important differences, Old Testament believers were on essentially the same basis with God as Christians are. We learn more of the relationship as we continue to study the Scripture.

e. *In types.* We have already considered these, and something of the way Christ is revealed in them. (See Chapter 15.)

f. *In direct prophecies.* These we have also looked at brief-ly. (See Chapter 19.)

The whole Bible, including the Old Testament Scrip-tures, is centered in Christ and bears witness to him (Jn. 5:39). He taught the disciples about himself from those Scriptures (Lk. 24:25-27) and rebuked them because they had not already understood something about him from the Scriptures. We should, therefore, seek to find Christ re-vealed in the Old Testament. But we should always use the New Testament to check what we find there since the New Testament gives the full revelation of him.

These first three points indicate a basic unity in the Bible: (1) Both Old and New Testaments are from God, (2) they reveal his redemptive plan (which is basically one plan) and (3) that plan is centered in Christ. The passages we have seen make it quite clear that the Bible gives one way of sal-vation, not two or more.

Points of Contrast
The New Testament also indicates, however, that some things in the Old Testament definitely contrast with the revelation of the New. There are, in fact, several points of contrast, though not all are of the same kind. There are probably at least three different kinds. First, there are con-trasts between the whole Old Testament period and New Testament times, including the revelation given by God in each. Second, there are contrasts between the Old Testa-ment law, or the Old Testament covenant with Israel as such, and the New Testament revelation of the New Cove-nant. Third, there is a contrast, even a contradiction, be-tween the Jewish misunderstanding of the old covenant as offering salvation by works and the New Testament revela-tion of God's way of salvation by faith.

This third type of contrast is not really between two things arranged by God. It is rather between man's under-standing and God's plan. The first three points in this chapter show that God does not have two opposite ways of salvation or ways of life. So we need not spend time now with the Jewish misunderstanding, though we do need to recognize it where we find it in Scripture. (Acts 15:7-11; Rom. 9:30—10:13; and Gal. 3 are passages that speak of it.) We will look at contrasts of the first two types, beginning with those that refer in general to the Old and New Testament periods.

1. *The Old and the New Ages*

Hebrews 7:16, 24, 28; 9:10 indicate a contrast relating to time. The Old Testament is for a time; the New is forever. The contrast is between that which is *temporary* and that which is *permanent,* or *final.*

Notice Mark 1:15; Galatians 4:3-4. What can be the force of *the time had fully come*? Doesn't it imply a time that was not full, a time of preparation? The New Testament sees the Old Testament period as that time. The world and the Jewish people had to be prepared for the coming of Christ. There is a contrast between *preparation* and *completion.*

Many passages in the New Testament (for example, Mt. 1:22; 2:17-18; 4:14-16; Acts 3:18, 21-24; 8:32-35; 13:27-29) speak of something spoken or written in the Old Testament as being fulfilled. There is a contrast between *prediction* and *fulfillment.*

Another contrast comes in these verses: Matthew 10:5-6; 15:24; Acts 3:26; 10:34-35; 18:5-6. In the Old Testament God's dealings were primarily with which nation? These New Testament verses show that now he is treating all nations alike. We can say, then, that the contrast is between *one nation* and *all nations,* or between Jews only and Jews along with Gentiles.

We can see still another clear contrast in Hebrews 7:19; 9:15; 10:4-7, 10, 14; 11:39-40. It is between that which is *partial,* or imperfect, and that which is *full,* or perfect. This perfection or imperfection has no direct reference to sin, as though now there is sinless perfection, but rather to the completeness of God's economy in the period.

2. *The Old and the New Covenants*

Besides the above contrasts that apply to the general periods of time, we can notice a few that refer more specifically to the Old Covenant and the New.

Look at Hebrews 8:5; 9:10-11; 12:18-24. Here the *earthly* (or materialistic) phase of the Old Covenant is contrasted with its *spiritual* counterparts in the New. There were earthly features that pointed forward or upward to spiritual realities. This contrast is not absolute, however; Hebrews 11:10, 16 and other passages show that the Old Testament believers also had spiritual and heavenly goals and hopes.

It is curious that another contrast seems to be the exact opposite of the one above. (See Heb. 8:2, 5; 10:1; Col. 2:16-17.) The material, earthly aspects of the Old Covenant are said to be a *shadow*, or copy, of the *real*, or true. The latter is in heaven, but is also revealed in the New Covenant. The tabernacle is contrasted both with the reality in heaven and with the spiritual reality that we can experience now, namely, the place of God's presence.

This is shown plainly in the ceremonial part of the Mosaic law. The instructions about offering sacrifices (Lev. 1—8), observing festivals (Lev. 23), constructing the tabernacle (Ex. 25—28) and following the ritual (Ex. 29—30) are a prominent part of them. Also, there are the laws of the social or civil code (such as Lev. 13 concerning leprosy and Lev. 25 concerning loans and slavery). Why don't we follow these laws now? Because we read New Testament passages such as Hebrews 9:11-14; 10:1-10; and see that the law was a shadow of the spiritual realities that Christ has established and that God has abolished the shadow. We now seek to follow the real. It may not always be easy to decide whether a particular Old Testament law or passage is part of the shadow only or has permanent validity, but the more we study his Word the more God will give us discernment about such things.

We notice a third contrast in Jeremiah 31:31, 34; Romans 8:3; and Hebrews 7:18—a contrast between *weakness* and *power*. This does not mean that God's power was not shown in the Old Testament. On the contrary, it was demonstrated, Scripture declares, many times. But the law God gave had a weakness: Man could not keep it. That fact is the basis for contrasting the law with the New Covenant, when God will put his law in men's hearts so that by the Spirit they can keep God's law.

Some Bible students see another contrast between the Old Covenant and the New, namely, that the Old is one of *law* and the New is one of *grace*. And they conclude that we as believers have nothing to do with the Ten Commandments since the Decalogue is part, perhaps the heart, of the Old Covenant.

How shall we approach this question? By studying the following references: Matthew 15:3-7; 19:17-18; Mark 10:19; Luke 4:8; 11:2; Romans 1:23; 2:24; 13:9; 1 Corinthians 5:11; 8:5-6; 10:14; Ephesians 4:25, 28; 5:3; 6:1-3; Colossians 3:5, 9; 1 Thessalonians 1:9; 1 Timothy 6:1; James 2:10-11; 4:2; 1 John 5:21; Revelation 13:6; 22:9.

These verses show that nine of the Ten Commandments are mentioned in the New Testament, especially in the Epistles. So they are part of the New Covenant, God's rule for us. God evidently expects us to obey them. One is not repeated, the fourth: "Remember the Sabbath day to keep it holy." Did the early church continue to keep the Sabbath? There is no evidence that they did, and some evidence indicates that the first day each week became the day they observed. (See Acts 20:7; 1 Cor. 16:2.)

Therefore, though the Ten Commandments were given to the Jews in the law, they are obviously God's permanent standards for his people. Even in the fourth, though the command is not repeated in the same form, a permanent principle of a "Lord's Day" seems clearly to be operative among the early Christians. And we remember that the seventh day was hallowed by God at the time of creation, long before the giving of the law. So, though we are under grace, we are also "under the law of Christ" (1 Cor. 9:21), and the permanent principles of God's moral law (starting with the Ten Commandments but including more) are God's will for us today. (See Chapter 22, No. 1.)

There is yet another contrast that many people see in the Bible, namely, that the morality of the Old Testament does not agree with that of the New—not only that people during the Old Testament period did not measure up to New Testament standards but also that sometimes they were not rebuked by God for their conduct.

In some cases it actually seems as if the laws given by God were lower than those of the New Testament. For instance, God commanded the Israelites to wipe out the Amalekites completely (Ex. 17:8-16). Other nations, too, were to be destroyed (as in Ex. 34:12-16 and Deut. 7:1-5). The Israelites were to make no treaty with the nations of Palestine, but to kill them or drive them out (as in Ex. 23:23-33). In some cases God plainly commanded even women and children to be killed (Deut. 20:16-18). It seems as though God was dealing harshly with people other than the Israelites; in any case, his action does not seem to fit in with the revelation of his love and mercy for all the world. How are we to understand this problem?

First, we must remember that the nations destroyed were morally corrupt; indeed, they had no standards of holiness and true worship. God did not seek to purify one nation because he loved its people more than others or because it was the biggest nation or because its people were more worthy than others. (See Deut. 7:7.) In fact, the Israelites, too, were without standards until God taught them. But because he chose this one people to become a righteous people they had to be segregated from the surrounding corruption.

Moreover, God had been patient with the other nations

for a long time. Long before the exodus, God had said, "The iniquity of the Amorites is not yet complete" (Gen. 15:16), which suggests that there is a completion of iniquity in a nation when it has refused to repent and turn from evil to God. Till that time God is patient and waits. When that point is reached he judges. And in some instances he used one nation to judge another by war and killing. It was necessary to do this with Israel's enemies because if they were not destroyed they would continue to corrupt Israel. Numbers 25:1-2; 31:1-20; and Judges 2:1-4 show clearly that this is what actually happened: Because the Israelites failed to destroy those nations, they were themselves corrupted by them.

It is not, then, that Israel took personal vengeance on its enemies or that God was playing favorites. His action was like a surgical operation that was necessary to remove some infection or some diseased portion from society. (See Chapter 18, No. 3, for a discussion of the so-called Imprecatory Psalms.)

Another puzzle is the fact that God permitted polygamy and "easy" divorce during the Old Testament period, but does not do so now. Spiritual leaders like Abraham and David had more than one wife (many in some cases) yet seemed to have no conviction that it was wrong and were not rebuked by God. God permitted Israelite men to separate from their wives simply by handing them "a bill of divorce" (Deut. 24:1-4).

This genuine problem does not have a simple answer, but we can get light on it from Matthew 19:3-9. There Christ explains why God allowed divorce in the Old Testament. Does Christ say that divorce was God's original plan? No. Then how does that original plan compare with the New Testament plan? He does not spell out the answer, but he indicates that God did not have more than one plan. Rather, from the beginning he had the high standard of monogamous marriage, one man and one woman.

Why did he tolerate a lower standard of life for the Old Testament period? "For your hardness of heart," Christ said. That is, the people could not take the higher standard. They were still learning other more important principles of life and worship, so God did not demand other things of them. He taught them gradually, as though they were children. His standard did not actually change, but he did for the time permit things that were neither the highest nor according to his standard.

There are other aspects of the moral standards and conditions during the Old Testament period which present problems of interpretation. In general they may be understood along the lines of the ones we have already considered. To sum up, we can keep in mind certain basic principles when we compare the morality of the Old Testament with that of the New.

a. *God revealed his will to man in a progressive way.* In the earlier period he did not reveal his complete standards as he later made them known through Christ and the apostles. (See Mt. 5:27-28 and Heb. 1:1-2.)

b. *In many instances what Old Testament saints did was not necessarily what God told them to do.* Even as we do, they also at times departed from God's will. (See 1 Kings 10:23, 26; 11:1-3, with Deut. 17:16-17.)

c. *God at times permitted things that he did not sanction.* In other words, he tolerated things that he did not approve. In some cases no disapproval by God is recorded. (See Mt. 19:3-9.)

d. *The violent, sometimes figurative language used in Old Testament poetry—often uttered with deep emotion and arising from strong concern for God's honor and truth—is not to be interpreted as if it were cold, literal prose.* (See Ps. 58:6.)

This has been a brief look at the relation of the Testaments. How shall we then regard the Old Testament? The New Testament teaches us. We see it as God's revelation: Just as much as the New, it is God's Word to us. In it we see

God's plan of salvation, the way God saves men and women by his grace and the way he changes them to become like Christ. For this the Old Testament reveals Christ in various ways and prepares for his coming. This unity helps us understand many Old Testament passages.

There are the contrasts also. We must not ignore them and lump everything together as though there are no differences. The New Testament helps us to recognize the kinds of contrast that exist. We therefore seek to find in the Old Testament both the temporary features and the permanent principles. And we read it for light on our own relation to God and for help with our growth in his grace.

IV

Personal Application

22 Responding to God's Word

We have looked at a number of principles, both general and specific, for Bible study and interpretation. I hope that you are eager now to begin some serious Bible study. Before you do, it would be well for you to read Chapter 6 again, noting carefully the suggestions for observing. These are quite important and will be a great help to you.

Before the study actually begins, we need to think carefully about the real goal of knowing the Word of God. For what purpose has God given us the Bible? God's Word itself tells us: that we may become children of God and live to his glory. The final end of understanding your Bible is living to the glory of God.

A person can learn a great deal about the Bible by a theoretical and technical study of it. But true understanding comes only when a person responds to the claims God makes upon him through the Word. The Bible has a spiritual dimension that can be grasped only when the will responds to what God says, not simply when the mind analyzes the language.

What, for example, does Romans 12:1 mean? We can analyze it and point out that *therefore* looks back to the first eleven chapters which tell of God's grace to us in Christ These chapters provide the ground of Paul's appeal

We can study the words *sacrifice* and *living,* connecting them with the Old Testament sacrifices that were dead. We can discover that a sacrifice is something completely devoted to God and interpret that we are to live out our devotion rather than die to demonstrate it. We can find other points and phases of meaning that the language reveals. But if all this is a purely theoretical exercise, we have not truly understood the passage. Only when we get all this meaning and also bow before the Lord in a real surrender of our body, and indeed our whole self, do we understand what Romans 12:1 means.

Theoretical knowledge of the Bible may well be what the Bible means by the letter or "written code" that kills (Rom. 2:29; 2 Cor. 3:6). Learning moral or spiritual truth without facing the moral or spiritual challenge it makes hardens our spirits. Since the truth of the Bible always makes a spiritual challenge, we must beware of treating the Bible as just another branch of human knowledge to be studied in the same way others are studied.

Furthermore, the demands of the Bible are authoritative, not optional. God does not merely make suggestions to us. He does not appeal, "Please, won't you consider doing this?" He commands, "Do this!" The only options we have are to obey or not. Obedience is the key to knowledge of the Bible.

Responding to God's Message

But not all God's message is given in the form of commands. It is not sufficient, therefore, to say that the correct personal application of the Bible is just to obey what God directly commands. The message requiring a response is given in various ways, and we must respond in different ways. Let us notice the appropriate responses we should make to the ways in which God speaks.

1. *By obeying God's commands and prohibitions:* God tells us something we are to do or not to do.

Some of his commands were given to an individual or group in a particular situation. For example, just before Pentecost Jesus told his disciples to "stay in the city, until you are clothed with power from on high" (Lk. 24:49). He gave this command at a certain point in history to a particular group of people. Or, during his ministry Jesus ordered a young man to "go, sell what you possess and give to the poor, . . . and come, follow me" (Mt. 19:21). The context indicates that the man's possessions were an idol and a barrier keeping him from following Christ. So Jesus said this to him, but he does not say it to everyone. (Compare Lk. 19:8-9.) Again, a man Jesus cured wished to remain with Jesus, but Jesus had other work for him. Hence, Jesus gave him this specific command: "Return to your home, and declare how much God has done for you" (Lk. 8:39).

A specific command may apply fully only to the one or ones to whom Jesus spoke; but a principle may lie at the root of the command, and the Holy Spirit may want us to apply that principle. For instance, Jesus told the young man to sell his possessions because they were a hindrance. The principle here may well be that everyone should rid himself of any hindrance to following Jesus. God may say this to every one of us. How do we apply it? We seek to obey.

Other commands of Scripture are more general, for instance, "Finally, my brethren, rejoice in the Lord" (Phil. 3:1). Also 1 Corinthians 10:31, "So, whether you eat or drink, or whatever you do, do all to the glory of God." And Proverbs 27:1, "Do not boast about tomorrow, for you do not know what a day may bring." There are hundreds of others. We should seek to interpret the language to get their true meaning, and then obey them.

Many passages (such as Jn. 14:15; Rom. 8:4; 1 Jn. 2:3; 5:3) show us that we are obligated to obey Christ's commands, that in fact such obedience shows our love for him. We are to fulfill the righteousness of God's law. Paul touches on this question, too (1 Cor. 9). In showing that he seeks to be all things to all men, he speaks of his relation to those who are without law. He seeks to be *as* without law, but quickly qualifies that he means "not being without law toward God but under the law of Christ" (v. 21). He does not mean that he is free from God's commands.

So God's laws are upon us. When we study the Old Testament laws, we must see which were only for that time and which are timeless. Even in the New Testament, there may be some commands that refer to a particular cultural situation in their literal form but contain a principle for all time. Consider John 13:14-15, where Jesus washed his disciple's feet and commanded them to follow his example. Some Bible students also consider the instructions about women's hair and head covering (1 Cor. 11:2-16) and about women keeping quiet in meetings (1 Cor. 14:33-35) to be of the same kind. (See also 1 Thess. 5:26.) These raise difficult problems, but we can all agree that when we understand a certain command as God meant us to understand it, our response should be to obey it gladly and wholeheartedly.

2. *By claiming his promises and avoiding his threats:* In his Word God sometimes indicates that he will do good or bless (a promise) or he declares that he will punish or inflict hurt (a threat). How shall we respond to the many passages that are of this nature?

First, we must recognize and understand the different kinds of promises and threats. Some are unconditional promises, where God says he will give some good thing regardless of how people act. For example, in Genesis 9:11 God says that he will never again destroy the earth with a flood. He does not say this depends on man's behavior; it is God's unconditional promise. We can accept and thank God for such promises, while continuing to study them carefully to be sure that they are truly unconditional. For, as we shall see, a condition may be present but not be clear and plain. (See also Gen. 15:14-16; Jer. 23:5.)

Most Bible promises seem to be conditional. God says, in

effect, that if people do or do not do certain things, he will bless.

These conditional promises are stated in different ways. Some are plain, open conditions, in which the promise is preceded or followed by *If you* or words to that effect. We cannot mistake the condition. (See Deut. 28:2-3; Rom. 10:9; Rev. 2:7.) Some are what we may call *indirect conditions* like 1 Samuel 2:30, "those who honor me I will honor." Surely this is the same as saying, "If someone honors me I will honor him," which is a conditional promise. In still other promises the condition is not in the same sentence but in the context or possibly in another passage. The verses surrounding Jeremiah 31:34 state the circumstances or conditions under which God will forgive the iniquities of his people. (Compare Ex. 23:25.) Isaiah 58 is another important example, for God gives several beautiful promises which are based on definite conditions found in the context.

If the promise is conditional, then we dare not claim it apart from the condition. The only right application is to study and accept the condition, seek to fulfill it and only then by faith rejoice in the promise.

We can also view the promises of the Bible as direct or indirect. Direct promises are obvious, such as "I will strengthen you" (Is. 41:10). Indirect promises are not so easily recognized. One is in Hebrews 10:34: "since you knew that you yourselves had a better possession and an abiding one." Some students may prefer to consider this a statement of fact rather than a promise, since it refers to what we have rather than what we will get. But since it refers to a heavenly possession contrasted with earthly property and since we do not fully enjoy that possession now but will in the future, we can regard this as an indirect promise.

Promises, whether direct or indirect, are to be understood by careful study, then prayerfully believed and claimed.

Threats are God's solemn declarations of his purpose to punish. He punishes man for what man does, for the sin man commits; therefore, in a sense, all threats are conditional. The terrible list of curses given by God in Deuteronomy 28 follows a shorter list of blessings. The blessings are introduced by *If you will diligently obey* and the curses by *If you will not obey.*

We can apply the threats to ourselves by seeking to understand the correct meaning of both the threat and its condition and then by obeying the condition, thus avoiding the threat.

3. *By learning from examples, both good and bad:* The Bible has many examples of righteousness, faith and other virtues as well as of sin and doubt. They are found mainly in the narrative sections of both the Old and New Testaments. Other sections, such as Paul's epistles, also contain some. We can learn from what Bible characters say about themselves, as well as from what is said about them. The psalmists and prophets give us examples by testimony, and so do Paul and Peter in their letters. (See Ps. 44:5-6; Phil. 1:21.)

Sometimes it is difficult to interpret the acts or words of Bible characters, that is, it is hard to know whether the example is good or bad. Were Paul and Barnabas both right or both wrong in their quarrel over Mark (Acts 15:36-41), or was one right and the other wrong? What about Paul's act in Acts 16:3 or in 21:26? Some students raise the same question about the Imprecatory Psalms. Is the example of the psalmist right or wrong? (See Chapter 18.) These passages are not easy to interpret and require careful, prayerful study.

We must seek to interpret each example, see the principle it contains and then apply the principle to our own situation. Consider Romans 2:17-25, for instance. Verse 25 speaks of the Jews' being circumcised and trusting in it, while possessing the law and not obeying it. The principle seems to be. You have God's revelation and the ordinance commanded in it, but if you disobey God's Word then this religious observance is of no value. We, too, have God's Word, and we also have religious observances, like baptism and the Lord's Supper. Is there spiritual profit in partaking of the Lord's Supper? Yes, implies this passage, if we are obeying the Word of God. Otherwise, no.

So biblical examples, including those in the Old Testament (1 Cor. 10:6, 11), are for us. We must seek to understand the spiritual principle shown in them and then by God's grace act accordingly.

4. *By believing God's statements of truth:* Many passages in the Bible contain no direct appeal, command or challenge, but rather just assert that something is truth. Commonly they make a statement about God, to which is attached an appeal or a comment on what man should do. John 4:24, "God is spirit, and those who worship him must worship in spirit and truth." (See also Ex. 19:4-6; Ps. 9:7-10; 81.) Some verses simply state the truth, without any appeal. (See Ex. 34:6-7; Ps. 8:1; 24:1-2.) Perhaps nearby verses mentioned an appeal or command that bears some relation to a stated truth but is not directly linked. (See Ps. 19:1-6; 97:1-6.) Often statements of truth tell what God has done for his people or for men in general. (See Ps. 44:2-3; 78.)

These statements do not become true by our believing or obeying them: They are true whether we believe them or not. Our first response is simply to accept them and thank God for them. However, our experience of their truth may depend on whether or not we act in accord with them. God is a forgiving God, ready to pardon, but my experience of forgiveness will depend on whether I repent of my sin, confess it and accept Christ's death as my ground of cleansing. There is a great necessity that we have childlike faith in accepting what the Bible says about God and about what he has done.

5. *By acting on the direct teachings:* God also gives us his message by direct teachings about things related to spiri-

tual experience, like life, salvation and holy living. (These are not really distinct from point 4 above, but that refers to direct teaching about God and his work.) These teachings will not be in the form of a direct command or exhortation, though such commands have in them much teaching also.

Consider 1 Corinthians 13, which deals with Christian love. Not once does Paul appeal, "You ought to love like this." He simply teaches, "This is what love is." But the indirect appeal and challenge is very strong. I sense immediately that this is what I ought to be, and, if I am not, then I must seek God's help to love as this chapter pictures love. What is my response to such teaching? First, I accept it as God's will for me. Then I seek to obey it, and that means I seek God for his strength.

Understanding Your Bible

In order to learn how to interpret God's Word we have looked at many things that a student of the Bible needs to know and do. When all is said and done, however, the first and basic requirement is a hunger for God's Word. Neither I nor any other man can give you this. If you have an unquenchable thirst to know God and his truth, you will read the Bible again and again and again until you are soaked in that truth.

I have sought to guide into profitable study the person who has this thirst. If you lack the deep conviction that God's Word is 100% true and 100% necessary for your life and if you in fact spend little or no time studying the Bible, go to God with David's prayer: "Create in me a clean heart, O God, and put a new and right spirit within me" (Ps. 51:10). Ask him to make this other prayer of David's true for you, too: "Oh, how I love thy law! It is my meditation all the day" (Ps. 119:97). Pray as you read; read as you pray.

Then know as you read that all your study will demand response to God. It will not be only the critical analysis of a